INSCOM Aviation Series

FLYING IN THE SHADOWS

Forging Aerial Intelligence for the United States Army

Thomas N. Hauser

U.S. Army Intelligence and Security Command
Fort Belvoir, Virginia, 2023

Library of Congress Cataloging-in-Publication Data

Names: Hauser, Thomas N., author. | United States. Army. Army Intelligence
   & Security Command, issuing body.

Title: Flying in the shadows : forging aerial intelligence for the United States Army /
   Thomas N. Hauser.

Other titles: Forging aerial intelligence for the United States Army | INSCOM aviation series.

Description: Fort Belvoir, Virginia : U.S. Army Intelligence and Security
   Command, 2023. | Series: INSCOM aviation series | In scope of the U.S.
   Government Publishing Office Cataloging and Indexing Program (C&I);
   Federal Depository Library Program (FDLP) distribution status to be determined
   upon publication. | Includes bibliographical references and index.

Identifiers: LCCN 2023049061 | ISBN 9798989394906 (trade paperback)

Subjects: LCSH: United States. Army. Army Intelligence & Security
   Command--History. | United States. Army--Aviation--History. | Aerial observation
   (Military science)--United States--History. | Military intelligence--United States--History.
   | Vietnam War, 1961-1975--Aviation. | Aerial reconnaissance--Korea (North)--History.

Classification: LCC UG1243 .H38 2023 | DDC 358.4/5830973--dc23/eng/20231023 |
   SUDOC D 101.2:AE 8/3

LC record available at https://lccn.loc.gov/2023049061

Contents

LEFT BANK Landing by Williams

My fellow aviators
and I were resolved
after the war to contribute
and improve aerial intelligence.

— C. COLLAT

Foreword

Toujours Enavant is a rather classic saying from the annals of basic warfare from time immemorial meaning "always out front." What could be more descriptive of a basic tenet of military intelligence and yet be so self-explanatory? Securing knowledge of the enemy is exactly the essence of why warfighters value military intelligence and have expanded their approach to it in the age of modern combat. Our Nation's wars have clearly provided us with the insight and the desire to embrace aviation for intelligence purposes, to secure the battlefield advantage today and in the future. Another key phrase to simplistically capture this new and sometimes overlooked dimension, but one that found its eventual home inside the Army's Military Intelligence Corps' vernacular, is the Electronic High Ground. This phrase was more than a statement of where we were as we operated and experimented in a new type of warfare in Southeast Asia; it also implied a technological component, which henceforth, was brought to bear. One of our true trailblazers, Colonel Dick Mitchell, so eloquently expressed these visionary words back in the 1960s. To those of us who understood his conception, the ideas behind his expression stuck and remain with us today. This ever-progressing requirement, since the Nation's Civil War, to see first, be first and battle with the odds in our favor stems from having the ability to get above the fray, look deep and deeper into the enemy's lines, unveil his locations, capture (and decipher) his communications, and track his movements.

In 1966, while serving my first tour in Vietnam, my desperate search for whatever available intelligence impressed upon me the importance of how aerial reconnaissance could be vectored more directly to support the ground combat units. After flight school and then serving as an aviator in Vietnam in 1969, I delved even deeper. I participated in a rotary-wing signals intelligence project called LEFT BANK and witnessed a rapid growth of single and multi-engine fixed-wing aerial direction-finding programs and systems such as LAFFING EAGLE and LEFT JAB......all collectively intended to make the difference as a game changer. Proof of their value was a clear-cut case, and the rationale for why the Army should vigorously pursue further developments to produce a better military-intelligence system caught my enthusiasm.

My goal was getting aerial collected intelligence to actionable levels in a timely manner, but it would require proof of concept as well as convincing key personnel of the merits of this approach. The challenge was keeping this objective in the forefront because Vietnam was considered a short-term, counterinsurgency type of war as opposed to a full force-on-force engagement, but I was not alone. My fellow aviators and I were resolved after the war to contribute and improve aerial intelligence. My raison d'etre guided my career as we stayed fixed on the partnership between intelligence and aviation while keeping pace with technologies as they emerged over the last sixty years. Within those years, I served thirty-one on active duty for the Army as an infantry officer, an intelligence officer and an aviator and had a follow-on career with Northrop Grumman. I hope that I did some justice to this new and emerging arena at a critical time. Assisting whenever possible, I watched the Army's intelligence structures expand to accommodate and, more importantly, integrate with dedicated aviation reconnaissance and surveillance assets.

The outcome was a reliable product, which has served the Army well to the present. In following on with this fragile but self-proving concept, the Army's continuance in airborne radio direction finding in the post-Vietnam era took a second and unquestionable leap forward with systems such as the AN/USD-9 GUARDRAIL and the AN/ALQ-33 QUICK LOOK for signals along with the AN/APS-85 system for imagery. Essentially, it is my view that the progress and results achieved to date with industry giants such as Northrop Grumman and General Dynamics in aerial intelligence sensors and their accompanying aerial platforms speak for themselves. They, in essence, set the stage for how we now more comprehensively collect and more dynamically provide this information to U.S. ground-force components, regardless of the type of warfare.

The soldiers and civilians have since moved on, but the undertaking goes on. In the pages that follow, these original people and their accomplishments are spared from vanishing into the dustbin of obscurity. Their actions should be viewed as an introduction to a new field of intelligence and a guide around the obstacles that hinder real progress. The major players include the aviators themselves, some of whom were trailblazers, leading the way for others to continue in this pursuit. I consider myself most fortunate to have been present among this group, making a contribution, albeit a small one when one visualizes the size and depth of today's aerial intelligence force in the Army.

Of course, quite obviously, even if the basic warfighting tenets remain constant, technology will improve. Therefore, staying abreast of ways to modernize for success against typical and atypical warfighting scenarios facing our Nation's forces today and in the future merely reinforces the need to keep pace. The reader will undoubtedly appreciate this point while keeping in mind the necessity of staying ahead of the power curve in a combined effort to optimize intelligence and aviation and, in essence, by so doing, synchronize their associated technologies.

This book captures our goal to improve the Army's aerial intelligence enterprise and to realize Colonel Dick Mitchell's original vision of the *Electronic High Ground* and operating it "always out front." I am gratified to see that much has been accomplished and that today's professionals continue to work toward this same goal.

Carlos M. Collat
Colonel, United States Army (Retired)

These works represent an attempt
to illuminate that which had been
restricted and only discussed in
confidence, to connect the various parts,
and to present a larger picture.—

Preface

This book, the first of three, investigates a brand of aviation that serves the intelligence requirements of the United States Army. It tells the story of an unusual group of soldiers and civilians who served as aviators, equipment operators, developers, and maintainers. During peacetime they advanced their field with cutting-edge technologies, sometimes with scant resources, and in wartime, the fruits of their labor proved indispensable. Yet, due to the sensitive nature of their work, the contributions of these professionals have received little attention. Only recently has the passage of time lifted enough of the cloud of secrecy. These works represent an attempt to illuminate that which had been restricted and only discussed in confidence, to connect the various parts, and to present a larger picture. What follows is the product of years of research and writing. Although its scope is large, I do not expect to have the last word on the subject. Like many undertakings of this sort, I found that my inquiry led me to more questions than answers, but with all hope, the narrative within these pages will lay fertile ground for further exploration.

Authors often compare bringing a book to life to parenting a child. Development is sometimes unpredictable, and perhaps control is only imagined. More to the point, neither children nor books are reared without the help of others. My regret is that so many have waited too long for this publication. At the start of this project, I had no background in aerial intelligence, which has led me to rely heavily on the advice and assistance of experts. In particular I must thank three individuals who made their knowledge and experience available to me on paper. Dennis Buley, an accomplished program engineer who passed away years ago, Richard Mitchell, a retired Army officer and aviator who recently passed away, and Carlos Collat, also a retired Army officer and aviator, have provided invaluable source material to this project. Their collections of writings, books, media material, presentations, and photographs were essential to my research. Of equal importance was Collat's availability for consultation. How could I have written this book without them?

Beyond knowledge of subject matter, support had to come in many forms. I am deeply indebted to Rebecca Raines for lending a keen eye in reviewing and editing my manuscript. Among her attributes, her professional background in Army organization and official history kept me straight with the intricacies of military force structure. It is never simple. Furthermore, I owe much to Catherine Clary-Brown who orchestrated the declassification review. It was a long process, involving many individuals and organizations. I am much obliged to Ron Young, the head of INSCOM Public Affairs. It took his support to get this book funded and certified. Finally, of course, this work was ever dependent upon the guidance and support from Command Historian Michael Bigelow and the INSCOM History Office.

A special thanks goes to James Gilbert, Dr. Joseph Frechette, Diana Paul, and Carlos Collat for donating their time to read this manuscript and provide feedback. I am also grateful to those who granted interviews, including John Thomas, Darell Lance, Robert Pitman, Doug Roberts, Bill Hauser, Mike Bunty, John Hyde, and Clark Sullins. Additionally, my gratitude extends to those who advised me on so many aspects of aerial intelligence: Alan Lindley, Mark Arterburn, Karen Kovach, Ray Newton, Robert Cotsonas, and Andrew Rodriquez. Finally, I would like to recognize the administrative, artistic, and technical assistance provided by Mary Laing, Sharon Thorpe, Jocelyn Broussard, and Joy Brathwaite. It has been a privilege to work with such a dedicated and professional group of people.

U-8 by Wayne Salge

Past and present,
Army AISR battalions and
companies have not just been units
of maneuver with aviators,
systems operators, and maintainers.
They have also been experimental
vehicles, interacting with
a host of program managers,
engineers, and technical
experts, for introducing
the latest technologies
to the field.—

Prologue

A century ago, aerial intelligence had undergone its first phase of rapid advancement precipitated by the First World War. Over the heavily shelled landscape of the Western Front, on the eve of an offensive, reconnaissance aircraft might have resembled a swarm of bees above a clover patch. Some observers worked with little more than telescopes and binoculars, while others had at their disposal the most advanced cameras of their day. By today's standards, their sensors—the means of collecting information—and aerial platforms—the means of delivering and operating sensors in the air—lacked sophistication, yet in concept the practitioners' methods and processes bear a remarkable similarity. Then and now, the implementation of new technologies requires new training, organizational expansion, and logistical support. When successful, technological innovation yielded a better intelligence product or improved the dissemination of timely information. These were common markers of progress in this field and build on a recurring theme in this narrative.

It was during the First World War that military intelligence (MI) and aviation had consolidated into a firm partnership.[†] Both fields had undergone rapid technological growth, and the United States Army had taken a chance on aviation as a means of intelligence gathering. Cameras, radios, and optical devices soon became priority equipment. Fitting these new assets within a system to satisfy wartime requirements necessitated hasty improvisation, which placed limits on forethought. Sometimes through nothing more than trial and error, the Army succeeded in establishing a successful aerial-intelligence force. This in itself was a learning experience. What came afterward was an acquisition cycle or a formalization of transforming innovation into useable military equipment.

---

† In recent decades, the definition of the term "military" has expanded to include all branches of the armed services. For the purpose of this book, the term is applied according to its original meaning. That is, exclusively to Army-related activity, and therefore, military intelligence is synonymous to Army intelligence but not to Naval, Marine, Coast-Guard, or Air-Force intelligence.

Following the war, aerial intelligence made steady advancement as a discipline in which transformation and innovation have since grown into subjects of intellectual importance. By their own definitions, they presuppose noteworthy changes in battlefield capability. More often than not, progress came out of numerous interconnected enhancements that perhaps in sum were equal to a single breakthrough. The Army benefited immensely from such minor improvements during the interwar period, and collectively, they paid incalculable dividends in the Second World War. The same pattern of progress continued to provide military advantages in the Cold War. In concrete terms, this form of intelligence had expanded from offering limited tactical awareness of the battlefield to providing an enhanced strategic overview by filling many niches from low-altitude artillery spotting to orbital imagery.

One of the few singular great leaps forward came with the development of airborne signals intelligence (SIGINT) in the 1960s. It began on a small scale with various forms of strategic collection, but a major sea change emerged out of necessity during the Vietnam conflict with the introduction of airborne radio direction finding (ARDF). Although the British and French had applied this concept experimentally against colonial uprisings, its substantive value was only demonstrated later when U.S. forces urgently required a system to track Marxist guerillas in Southeast Asia. What began as improvisation had become a large-scale endeavor. With greater U.S. involvement, it was not long before the airspace over Vietnam bore a resemblance to that over the trenches during the First World War, as numerous ARDF aircraft flew overhead in what again might have looked like a swarm, collectively identifying enemy targets. By the late 1960s, the Army and the United States Air Force required joint coordination to manage the high volume of air traffic from ARDF systems alone. Its success also induced greater development in other forms of airborne-SIGINT collection that would prove even more effective and would leave a legacy of programs that continue to this day.

Naturally, the Army did not miss its opportunity to apply the advancements gained from Vietnam to other missions in different theaters, and an airborne-SIGINT boom sparked a completely new way of approaching tactical intelligence much in the same way that aerial reconnaissance had done after the First World War. ARDF began as a means to avert mission failure in Vietnam, but it also introduced a new form of aviation as an MI discipline suited for the Cold War. Combined with the improved application of imagery intelligence (IMINT), ARDF and airborne-SIGINT collection proved indispensable along the static militarized borders, demarcating east and west. It was in this period of transition that these disciplines matured in time to help uncover a menacing buildup in the Korean theater, which could have led to war if left unchecked. This success was the first significant accomplishment of the newly organized U.S. Army Intelligence and Security Command (INSCOM), and more important, it secured momentum behind building more aerial programs.

Meanwhile, INSCOM and other command authorities in the Army had to redefine doctrine and organization as new systems came online. This necessitates a commitment to precise definitions and clear understanding. To the uninformed, for example, intelligence may appear almost identical to information under a cloak of secrecy. To those in the field, however, it is better understood as a subset of information—identified, collected, analyzed, and disseminated—to aid the decision making of military commanders or policy makers. In this way, reconnaissance is also different from intelligence because it is an act of gathering information to answer a specific military question. Even so, reconnaissance is important to intelligence as a supplier of useful information. Surveillance—the persistent monitoring of a target or targets—informs intelligence too. In the last three decades, the Army has combined these three functions—now called aerial intelligence, surveillance, and reconnaissance (AISR)—to support each other within the aviation field.

In light of the events that transpired and the challenges leading up to

INSCOM, this book traces the development of aerial intelligence for the Army and underscores its effectiveness as a countermeasure during the Vietnam conflict, thereafter engendering its rapid growth and success as a military discipline in the post-war period. Similar to progress preceding the First World War, technologies had matured by the 1960s to spark a new wave of aerial-intelligence innovations, only requiring a military exigency to render implementation.

This sets the stage to narrate the formative years of the Army's long venture into aerial intelligence. The reader may infer that early development was a struggle uphill due to the unusual problems facing this nontraditional military discipline. The pioneers, whether aviators, operators, engineers, or technicians, had to be flexible in mind as well as dedicated to create the forerunner of modern medium-altitude AISR, which has proven indispensable in our two most recent conflicts in Southwest Asia.

Finally, in the larger context, the purpose of this book—and two more that will follow in a series—is twofold: first, to explain how and why INSCOM started in 1977 with one aviation company and then found itself three decades later with all of the AISR units in the Army, and second, to explore the challenges of MI aviation while tracing the evolution of its systems and organizations. Past and present, Army AISR battalions and companies have not just been units of maneuver with aviators, systems operators, and maintainers. They have also been experimental vehicles, interacting with a host of program managers, engineers, and technical experts, for introducing the latest technologies to the field. But in the numerous volumes that cover so much of military intelligence, the topic at hand has not received any careful, singular treatment. It is to fill this gap that defines the purpose of these works. If the efforts of those who contemplated and toiled to build a future for MI aviation are brought into light, then this writing will not be considered in vain.

*Starting in the late eighteenth century, technology
and industrialization transformed warfare, which allowed military
professionals to imagine the high ground in new ways.
It should not be surprising, therefore, that surveillance from the air was born
out of these imaginings and prospered through material progress.—*

The Union Army Balloon Corps prepares to launch the balloon Intrepid during the Battle of Seven Pines.

CHAPTER ONE

The Origins of Aerial Intelligence, Surveillance, and Reconnaissance

The Dawn of an Era: Aerial Observation

Since the advent of warfare, military leaders have gone to great lengths to obtain a clear perception of their enemy on the battlefield. To that end, securing the high ground not only improved tactical advantage but also awarded a bird's eye view of an opponent's position and fighting capability. Starting in the late eighteenth century, technology and industrialization transformed warfare, which allowed military professionals to imagine the high ground in new ways. It should not be surprising, therefore, that surveillance from the air was born out of these imaginings and prospered through material progress. Although technology presented as many logistical hindrances as tactical opportunities in the early years of aerial observation, the next advancement was never far away to spur inventive military thinking toward a new way of securing the high ground.

To this point, we may place the origins of aerial intelligence at the forefront of the industrial age. Only ten years after the Montgolfier brothers had launched the first hot-air-balloon flight in 1783, the French Army had two full companies dedicated to this new

A Union Army balloon in ascension.

Spectators were undoubtedly impressed with the Army's initial test of the Wright brothers' Wright Flyer over Fort Myer, Virginia.

aerial platform. Although less than effective over battlefields of that day, the tethered balloon ignited the restless imagination of military innovators. The eighteenth century, however, was not to be the prime time for this form of observation. The balloon's potential advantages were more than offset by logistical problems. The necessary heavy equipment needed to produce hot air or transport hydrogen impeded mobility. Decades later, when support equipment became less cumbersome, the employment of balloons in the American Civil War, the Spanish American War, and the First World War proved that they could effectively collect intelligence, but tactical vulnerability limited their application on the battlefield. Nevertheless, the balloon illuminated the potential of aerial observation when invention would yield new platforms of ascension.

The successful flight of a fixed-wing aircraft by the Wright brothers in 1903 marked a technological revolution in aviation and consequently for aerial intelligence. The U.S. Army Signal Corps, then responsible for military aviation, soon became interested in the Wrights' invention. In response to specifications issued by the Signal Corps in 1907, the Wrights developed an aircraft suitable for military use.[1] In September 1908, Orville Wright delivered a prototype to Fort Myer, Virginia.[2] The ensuing tests clearly revealed that heavier-than-air flight had possibilities, but there were hazards. Orville Wright's last test flight in front of evaluators ended in a crash, not only severely wounding him but killing his passenger, Lieutenant Thomas E. Selfridge, who thus became the Army's first aviation fatality. The tragedy, however, did not dissuade the Signal Corps from purchasing a Wright Flyer in 1909. Wilbur Wright provided the initial flight instruction.[3]

Enthusiasm ran high among signal officers as they quickly developed a new doctrine for aerial

Aerial photographers with camera equipment as seen from the rear cockpits of their Army observation aircraft.

observation, codified in Field Service Regulations, 1910.[4] Only one year later, with a handful of qualified pilots, the Army established its first aviation school at College Park, Maryland. Field Service Regulations, 1914 assigned a passive reconnaissance role to aviation, which aided in defining the mission of the newly created Aviation Section of the Signal Corps.[5]

The American entry into the First World War along with a boom in technological development opened numerous opportunities to expand aerial reconnaissance. As Army historian Edgar Raines noted,

STUDY OF 1ST - 2ND - 3RD TRENCH SYSTEMS

During World War I, the analysis of airborne photography quickly developed into an elaborate system.

"[u]nder the stimulus of war, aircraft had become infinitely more powerful and aviation doctrine, like those of other branches, complex and specialized."[6] American airplanes flew directly over enemy lines to acquire the missing pieces of the intelligence puzzle. Sustained surveillance required blanketing the front with a mass of aerial observers.

Photography was the most frequently used method of aerial collection. Cameras provided intelligence staffs with a multitude of images to determine the location and strength of enemy positions for the attack as well as to deduce enemy intentions by examining changes in the rear. Under the right conditions, these missions returned visual evidence of hitherto concealed enemy troop concentrations. The photographs themselves became pieces of a complex mosaic when analysts arranged them on enlarged pinup boards to survey broad sections of the front. In addition, with so much artillery fire, ground observers had difficulty judging the impact of a barrage. For clarification, regular photographic missions allowed staffs to examine the progress of map-firing, which became a common artillery technique during World War I.

The war produced the first air campaigns and thereby the first large-scale reconnaissance and surveillance efforts. The flyers, photographers, and analysts could boast success by the latter part of 1918. In one offensive operation, the Army's film-development sections produced and distributed 56,000 prints in four days. Between 15 and 17 July 1918, airborne photography allowed three American divisions to anticipate and halt a German attack against Paris across the Marne River. By the time of the Armistice in November 1918, aerial reconnaissance was used unsparingly, and American photographic equipment had technologically surpassed that of Britain and France.[7]

Advancements in the Interwar Period and Second World War

In 1926 Congress passed the Air Corps Act, which effectively unified aviation elements in the Army into one organization, named the U.S. Army Air Corps. With regard to intelligence, air officers were incorporated into the Military Intelligence Division of the Army Staff, and the air attaché took his place alongside naval and military attachés. As a result of the efforts of Lieutenant George Goddard, who would become the renowned pioneer of aerial observation and a brigadier general in the Air Force, airborne photographic and mapping units remained cutting edge by implementing a series of first-time innovations: the film strip camera, photo-composite maps of American cities, and different types of lenses for night-aerial, high-altitude, and stereoscopic photography.

Pursuing other uses of aerial reconnaissance, artillery officers in the 1930s were attempting to acquire a light, inexpensive, but hardy, aircraft from the domestic market such as one produced by the Piper Aircraft Company. The acquisition of this type of airplane, however, did not come easily for a variety of reasons. Perhaps reflecting the difficulty in communications between air and artillery crews during training exercises, Air Corps Commander, General Oscar Westover, and later General Henry H. Arnold, preferred more sophisticated aircraft, ignoring the requirements of the artillery spotter.[8] Indeed, the only common ground between the Air Corps and Artillery Branch was a fascination for the autogiro— a rotary-wing aircraft—which proved a premature technology after two years of failed experimentation. The artillery commanders' needs were finally recognized in 1937, when, observing the success of the German low-speed, high-wing monoplane, the Fiesler Storch, the Army Staff saw the need for a comparable design. After four years, however, the American attempt to copy the Fiesler Storch became bogged down in paperwork and design delays. The problem was exacerbated when

Photo interpreters during World War II.

the ground arms branch also pushed to copy another German-designed aerial platform, the helicopter, which led to only more false starts and delays. Impetus to finish the project only came after the American entry into the Second World War.[9]

With a few helpful advocates, such as Major General George S. Patton, who purchased his own small airplane and used it in field exercises, the Army settled on acquiring the Piper Cub J-3 as a tactical artillery spotter. For military purposes it was designated as the O-59 Grasshopper (later reclassified as the L-4), but many of its pilots would remember it as the "puddle jumper." Furthermore, the Army Staff concluded in 1941 that observation assets should be organic to field units and not directly under the purview of the Army Air Corps. By 1942, as the Army was reorganizing for its campaigns in World War II, General George C. Marshall, the Army Chief of Staff, had made the O-59 organic to infantry and armor divisions in addition to artillery. The aircraft also performed 30 percent of the general intelligence support missions in the European theater of World War II.[10]

Meanwhile, the field of airborne photography continued to advance. In the summer of 1939, the Army authorized a three-month course of instruction to grow a technical pool of expertise. Contributors included the Corps of Engineers for the instruction of topography. In 1941, Frederick Sonne, a founder

An L-4 observation aircraft, on a mission for the Ninth Army, flies low over Alsdorf, Germany.

of the Chicago Aerial Survey Company, perfected the S-2 Strip Camera for low-altitude, high-speed photography. It eliminated the need for a shutter and synchronized the exposure time of the film with the velocity and altitude of the aircraft. Goddard developed a camouflage detection film that made natural chlorophylls show up in a red coloring. Regardless, the Army's investment amounted to little more than a handful of reconnaissance units until bombs fell on Pearl Harbor.[11]

World War II was an opportunity for aviation to prove its newly developed, multifaceted capability in military intelligence. Army commanders and their staffs in Europe and the Pacific came to rely on the tactical picture coming from the complex, mosaic overlay composed of aerial photographs. Mobile engineer topographic battalions (one assigned to each corps) were the direct beneficiaries of airborne photographic intelligence; their maps were essential for any offensive. Long-range reconnaissance missions regularly identified where supplies were moving to betray enemy offensives and counteroffensives. On 17 November 1944, for instance, night photographic reconnaissance missions over railroad yards in Germany revealed a concentration of enemy divisions in a prelude

Allied forces in Korea retreat in the wake a Chinese surprise attack.

to the Battle of the Bulge. This information was critical when Lieutenant General Patton made his decision to maneuver the Third Army in anticipation of the German advance through the Ardennes Forest in December 1944.[12]

The Beginning of the Cold War

After World War II, the return to normalcy proved short-lived. The fall of the Axis powers gave rise to the Soviet Union and its satellites, known as the Warsaw Pact. When the threat of Soviet aggression in Eastern Europe and communist subversion in Western Europe became all too evident, the United States moved to action. The National Security Act of 1947 established the Air Force as a separate service, and the secretary of the air force answered directly to the newly created civilian secretary of defense. This reorganization profoundly affected aerial intelligence, surveillance and reconnaissance within all services.

Following a brief period of postwar contraction, most remaining aerial-intelligence assets went to the Air Force, most notably observation for strategic bombing, but it was not long before defense planners realized that such a strategically oriented service could not be an exclusive provider to tactical customers. Ground commanders found that they needed reporting from the air, not subject to inter-service competition for resources and not mired by a circuitous chain of communications. The Army thus retained observation aircraft for tactical intelligence and artillery spotting.

The restructuring of defense also changed the organization of signals intelligence (SIGINT). During World War II, SIGINT had been split between the Signal Security Agency under the Signal Corps and the theater commanders, but the arrangement proved problematic in later years. The Army Staff could not

The official seal of the Army Security Agency.

neatly separate strategic and tactical intelligence. As a solution, on 15 September 1945, the War Department merged the Signal Security Agency with tactical elements to form the U.S. Army Security Agency (ASA). This new organization, independent of the Signal Corps and directly subordinate to the War Department (and later the Department of the Army and the Army Assistant Chief of Staff for Intelligence) in Washington, DC, would eventually represent a significant part of aerial intelligence by integrating SIGINT equipment with aircraft to create innovative systems.

The first test of the new arrangement occurred in 1950 at the start of the Korean War. Unfortunately, military intelligence proved inadequate. In that field, within a span of only six months, the Army endured two major failures. The initial North Korean invasion came as a complete surprise as did the later Chinese intervention. Indeed, the head of United Nations Forces on the peninsula, General Douglas MacArthur, even conducted his own visual reconnaissance over North Korea, without seeing the Chinese Army poised for attack in November 1950. The U.S. Army could only improvise, and as the war continued, the problems persisted. General James Van Fleet, who took command of the U.S. Eighth Army in 1951, commented after the armistice in 1953 that there were still deficiencies in aerial observation and photography along with the operational system itself and remarked that "our intelligence operations in Korea have not yet approached the standards that we reached in the final year of the last war."[13]

The revelation of these moribund capabilities triggered reform and eventually led to a watershed in the development of Army aerial reconnaissance. Although the Korean War itself was largely fought using the equipment of World War II, which included the light artillery-spotting airplanes (improved

The 7th Infantry Division uses a road in Korea as a makeshift runway. Utility aircraft such as the L-5 proved versatile as visual and photographic reconnaissance aircraft.

versions of the Piper Cub) organic to the division, the need to meet a new—and somewhat arcane—threat behind the Iron Curtain spurred a concerted effort to harness scientific achievements into practical technologies. As a case in point, in 1953, the Army became involved in Project MICHIGAN—a research and development program in which scientists and engineers dedicated themselves to designing new military equipment. This included aerial drones carrying television cameras for observation and targeting at ranges of up to 200 miles.[14] As INSCOM historian John Finnegan noted, "[t]he new technologies under development would have a profound impact on the structure of Army intelligence in the years that followed."[15]

Through the 1950s, the Department of Defense reduced the size of the Army to eleven divisions. Soviet expansion shifted from building military forces on the Eurasian continent to arming proxies (such as Egypt and Cuba) worldwide. The smaller force, new political dynamic, and concerns of surprise attack led to a greater reliance on aircraft. Thus began the upgrade of the Army's aviation assets on a perpetual basis, encouraging near constant innovation. By 1960, there were 5,000 aircraft in its inventory, many of which were helicopters.[16]

These recently developed heliborne airframes had become a viable utility vehicle, first used for medical evacuation (memorable in the television show MASH) during the Korean War. Artillery and intelligence officers had long awaited the advent of improved rotary-wing vehicles to replace their fixed-wing aircraft. As the helicopter became more prominent, Army aviation at the division level, in accordance with the "New Look" of the Eisenhower administration, was consolidated into company-size units, which would eventually become battalions in the next decade. As part of this structure,

An early G-134 prototype; the t-tail was later replaced with vertical stabilizers.

observation helicopters became an integral part of division-level artillery. Not long after, scout versions, known as air cavalry, were assigned to reconnaissance battalions.

All the same, the acquisition of helicopters by no means signaled a decline in fixed-wing aircraft. In 1954, the Army and the United States Marine Corps agreed to design and construct a "joint service high performance aircraft for observation, artillery spotting, reconnaissance, command and utility use."[17] Designated as the G-134, the project went to the Grumman Aircraft Engineering Corporation for design and production. Despite the withdrawal of the Marine Corps, which wanted an uncomplicated spotter aircraft, the Army received a prototype, known as the YAO-1AF, a multi-functional, twin-engine aircraft with multiple reconnaissance capabilities. Its initial flight occurred on 14 April 1959.[18] In contrast to what the Marines would have wanted, the Army had plans to equip this new reconnaissance aircraft with payloads containing several types of sophisticated sensors under development at that time. It went into testing as the AO-1 "Mohawk."[19]

Grumman delivered nine prototypes between April 1959 and March 1960, and Fort Rucker, Alabama, opened a formal flight training program in April 1961.[20] In that month, the Mohawk dazzled spectators at the Paris Air Show by demonstrating a short landing and turning within a 355-foot radius.[21] The aircraft, however, sometimes proved fatal to test pilots who were not accustomed to the power of its turboprop engines. Consequently, it was known among them as "the Widow Maker." Future Mohawk aviators came to respect this aircraft not only for its capabilities but also for its flying

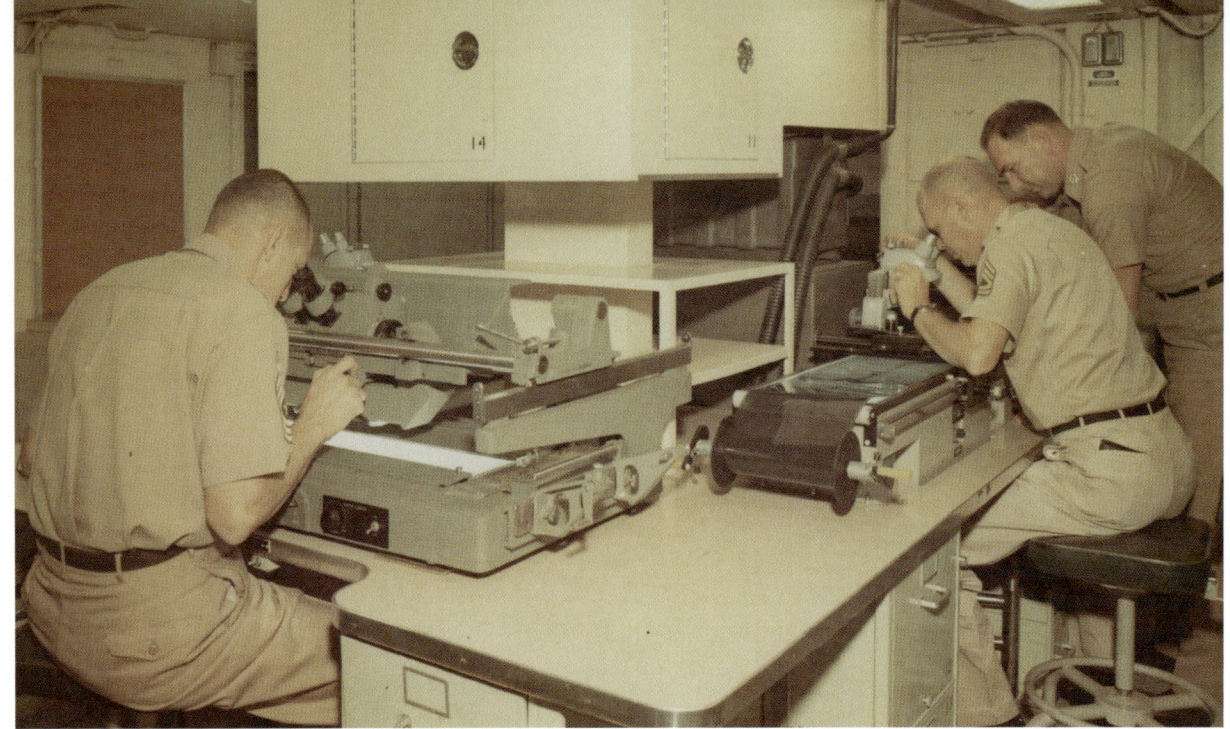

The Army's investment in airborne imagery analysis yielded a complex of interpretation facilities with the latest equipment, scattered across the National Capital Region.

challenges. In 1962, denoting its special attributes, the Mohawk's nomenclature became OV-1 (O standing for observation and V for vertical/short takeoff and landing).[22]

The OV-1 was also part of the Army's effort to remain relevant in photographic intelligence or PHOTINT, which had primarily been an aerial reconnaissance mission. At the start of the Cold War, the Army had only a few assets capable of accessing and analyzing national-level imagery on high-altitude Air Force platforms. The remedy for this shortfall came on 15 March 1955 through the establishment of the Photographic Interpretation Center. Its headquarters was located at Fort Holabird, Maryland, but analytical elements were scattered around the metropolitan area of the District of Columbia. Having secured its strategic need, the Army then proceeded to build an analytical capability for tactical airborne PHOTINT. The first unit of this type in the United States was the 1st Air Reconnaissance Support Battalion, organized on 1 February 1957 and stationed at Fort Polk, Louisiana.[23]

For photographic interpreters, the military force structure was not an easy fit at first. Access to imagery at the national level was problematic, and most of their duties in the continental United States consisted of either training, administration, or housekeeping, often leaving them with a feeling of inadequacy. The introduction of new technologies over time eventually improved their positions. In the coming years, interpreters dealt with a diverse assortment of products outside of conventional photography, such as infrared (IR) and radar images, leading to the expansion of their field into a broader discipline called

The EA-3B was the ELINT version of the Navy Douglas A-3 Skywarrior.
The aircraft initially served the Navy as a carrier-based bomber.

imagery intelligence (IMINT). The OV-1 Mohawk, as a dedicated reconnaissance and surveillance aircraft, was designed to accommodate this new source of intelligence. It could be equipped with airborne cameras, side-looking radars, or IR sensors. Indeed, radar sensing and IR detection redefined tactical aerial surveillance in the 1960s. Following the introduction of these technologies, the Photographic Interpretation Center was redesignated as the U.S. Army Imagery Interpretation Center in 1964. Henceforth, IMINT replaced PHOTINT as an operative term.[24]

Electronic intelligence or ELINT was also becoming more significant. Going back to World War II, ELINT had consisted primarily of radar detection and deception. In the 1950s, the U.S. had far more sophisticated radar systems and communications jamming—also known as Electronic Warfare (EW).

SAD-1 prepares its EA-3B for a mission.

By 1953, two ELINT processing centers were established. Initially, the Signal Corps, as the Army communications branch, had responsibility for ELINT and EW development and deployment. Two years later, in 1955, these functions, due to their sensitive nature, were consolidated under the authority of ASA.

This transfer of responsibility opened the door to a number of new joint aerial-intelligence ventures, such as a collaboration between ASA and the United States Navy to collect telemetric data on the launches of Soviet intercontinental ballistic missiles. Beginning in late 1958 and lasting until 1974, members from both services worked side by side in joint units.[25] ASA dubbed the overall project FARM TEAM (SEA BRINE in the Navy). The Navy provided the pilots and aerial platforms, Douglas

BATTLEAXE on a modified OV-1B Mohawk.

A3D-2Q (later EA-3B) aircraft— twin-engine (J-57 jets)—medium range attack bombers, reconfigured for special reconnaissance. The aircraft and crews were placed in two naval air units, named VQ-1 and VQ-2.

ASA operators formed their own units called Special Activities Detachments (SADs), each with approximately twenty system operators. They were assigned to U.S. Army Security Agency (USASA) SAD-1 and SAD-2, which were attached to VQ-1 and VQ-2 respectively.[26] SAD-1 was chartered to conduct "special Flight Operations" as directed by the commanding general of USASA, Pacific, based out of Atsugi Naval Air Station in Japan. The detachment flew missions from locations in the Pacific, including Shemya (Alaska), Guam, Midway Island, Johnston Island, Hawaii, and the Philippines. SAD-2 fell under the command of USASA, Europe. Based at Ramstein Air Force Base, West Germany, VQ-2 frequented the Canary Islands and Rota, Spain.[27]

The BATTLEAXE patch of Detachment 14.

The success of FARM TEAM encouraged ASA to make some modest investments in airborne SIGINT to support field stations in Europe. In 1961, ASA developers adapted one of the early prototype Mohawks (later replaced by an OV-1B Mohawk in 1962) as an aerial platform for an experimental ELINT program. The first installment was called HOT PIPE. The Mohawk was stripped of its dive brake mechanisms to reduce weight for the installation of electronic gear in its belly bay. Technicians mounted tubs underneath the fuselage to hold x-band antennae flush on its sides. The scopes and recording cameras were mounted in the observer's side of the cockpit. Through modifications, later iterations were known as BATTLEAXE and SILVER LANCE. (Missions flew until the late 1960s.) The systems and related personnel were assigned to Detachment 14, 318th ASA Battalion, at Field Station Herzogenaurach, located near the West German cities of Nuremberg and Erlangen. Most flights routinely originated out of Furth Army Airfield on the outskirts of Nuremberg.

Using a prototype Doppler navigation system, the observer could track his relative position at all times. With that information, he could plot the emitter locations of Soviet antiaircraft artillery and surface-to-air-missile sites from an analysis of his camera data at the field station. Flight paths followed closely along the eastern border of West Germany under constant monitoring by Air Force ground control to avoid straying into Warsaw Pact territory. In fact, Soviet jets often shadowed HOT PIPE/BATTLEAXE/SILVER LANCE flights on the other side of the border, and during tense situations, the Air Force called in F-104 Starfighters to provide an armed escort. The crews needed no reminder of their close proximity when they routinely detected the all-too-familiar radar locks from Soviet fire control.[28]

As the SILVER LANCE program was coming to an end, Field Station Herzogenaurach received another experimental system in 1966. The U.S. Army Electronic Warfare Laboratory (EWL), a part of the U.S. Army Electronics-Command at Fort Monmouth, New Jersey, modified a CV-2 Caribou to carry a system called SURE THING, later renamed GOFER DELTA, using commercial or off-the-shelf equipment to provide ELINT and communications intelligence (COMINT) coverage at specified frequencies. The aircraft was specially equipped with an autopilot linked to a Doppler navigation system. Whenever ASA required follow-up information in response to the detection of unusual SIGINT activity across the border, the field station would engage SURE THING using the

GOFER DELTA on the CV-2 Caribou aerial platform.

appropriate linguists provided by the 318th ASA Battalion. Despite modifications, the technology proved unreliable, which eventually led ASA to cancel the system prematurely. The Caribou later became an Air Force utility aircraft.[29]

By the early 1960s, the partnership between aviation and intelligence had become an Army legacy. The world wars were a testimony of success. Moreover, as conflicts in the Cold War became more complicated, aerial intelligence took on a greater importance during peacetime. In the years to come, politics in the Cold War would manifest itself as indirect conflict in isolated regions of the world. The Army would have to become even more innovative with aerial intelligence to protect American and allied interests.

The first ARDF fix made in combat, occurring on 27 May 1962,
vectored U.S. artillery onto a Viet Cong encampment,
inflicting four-hundred enemy casualties.—

Uncounted VC and NVA had their morning rice mixed with artillery,
fired on coordinates provided by IR equipped Mohawks.
Trucks on the Ho Chi Minh Trail, vessels at sea and encampments under
seemingly impenetrable jungle all were Mohawk targets.
—P. Reed

The versatility of the UH-1 or "Huey" made it suitable
as a U.S. Army aerial platform for search-and-destroy missions.

CHAPTER TWO:
Vietnam: A Watershed for Army Aerial Intelligence

The Early Stages

The 1960s witnessed a major shift in Cold War politics. The Kennedy and Johnson administrations abandoned the Eisenhower administration's New Look national security policy, relying on "massive retaliation," in favor of Flexible Response, a strategy designed to give the President more options against Soviet aggression. This policy change represented more than a shift in strategy; it reflected the symmetrical development of weapons in the ongoing arms race. As the Soviets sought weapons parity with the United States, a perceived missile gap led many American politicians to fear a Soviet nuclear response under aggravated political tensions. President John F. Kennedy's solution was to build a larger conventional army, primarily in Europe, that would give military and civilian leaders a gradation of responses in the event of an escalating conflict and thus buy time to allay a crisis. A larger and more versatile Army also facilitated intervention in proxy wars, one of which was mounting in Vietnam. This new stance heralded a new role for aerial intelligence.

New technologies blended well with traditional intelligence collection assets in Vietnam. Helicopters inserted remote-controlled SIGINT collectors, wiretapping devices, unattended ground sensors, and "people sniffers" deep in the jungles.[1] Infrared sensors and side-looking airborne radar provided a necessary supplement to the standard optical methods of surveillance and targeting. Furthermore, combining observation and armed helicopters in "pink teams" that had the dual mission of locating and fighting the enemy added a new dimension to aerial reconnaissance.[2] At the nucleus of operations, the J2, Military Assistance Command-Vietnam (MACV), maintained an automated intelligence database and oversaw collection management procedures. The most profound and successful development in aerial intelligence and targeting, however, emerged out of SIGINT-based airborne radio direction finding (ARDF) under ASA's command. Success in this effort led ASA to develop its own air arm.

At the start of American involvement, it was not apparent that aviation would take on any operational

A mobile DF team operates a vehicle-mounted PRD-1 to obtain an exact fix on an enemy station.

imperative in Vietnam. U.S. troops only trickled into the country after Kennedy approved the deployment of advisors on 9 May 1961. Fortunately for the American force, ASA had better prepared and equipped its units than at any other previous time. In addition to its primary mission of maintaining an array of field stations throughout the world, ASA had an effective doctrine for supporting combat troops, an ability to develop and operate new systems, and a mechanism for sustaining a highly qualified force. It was at this point that Major General John Willems, the Assistant Chief of Staff for Intelligence, alerted Major General William Breckinridge, commanding ASA, to plan for a deployment.[3]

An initial attempt to configure ARDF in an Army H-19 utility helicopter ended in failure. This prototype system is identifiable by its large antennae, extending perpendicular to the fuselage on each side of the platform.

Under Operations Plan 7-61, the vertical structure of ASA facilitated the expeditious assembly of a battalion-sized element called the 400th U.S. Army Security Agency Operations Unit (Provisional) to undertake the mission of supporting troops in Vietnam. ASA soldiers were predisposed to recognize the unit by its cover designation—the 3d Radio Research Unit (RRU). The South Vietnamese government had already reported success using U.S. COMINT equipment; however, when the 3d RRU arrived as the first full unit deployed in Vietnam, ASA operators quickly learned that all such claims were little more than exaggerations.[4]

Terrain determined the signal environment. Covered with dense foliage, the hilly, mountainous landscape of South Vietnam impeded broadcast bands that relied on a direct line of transmission. The best method of communication for the guerrilla fighters, therefore, was high-frequency (HF) propagation. Their transmitters were connected to horizontal radiating antennae that projected signals to ground receiving stations by reflecting signals off the ionosphere in the upper atmosphere.

In such an environment, the 3d RRU had a simple mission: pinpoint the enemy's headquarters by determining the origin of his HF radio communications that direct troop movements. The 3d RRU established a few semi-permanent direction-finding sites to form a net that could determine target areas of five to thirty miles in radius—an area too large for combat operations. To narrow down these

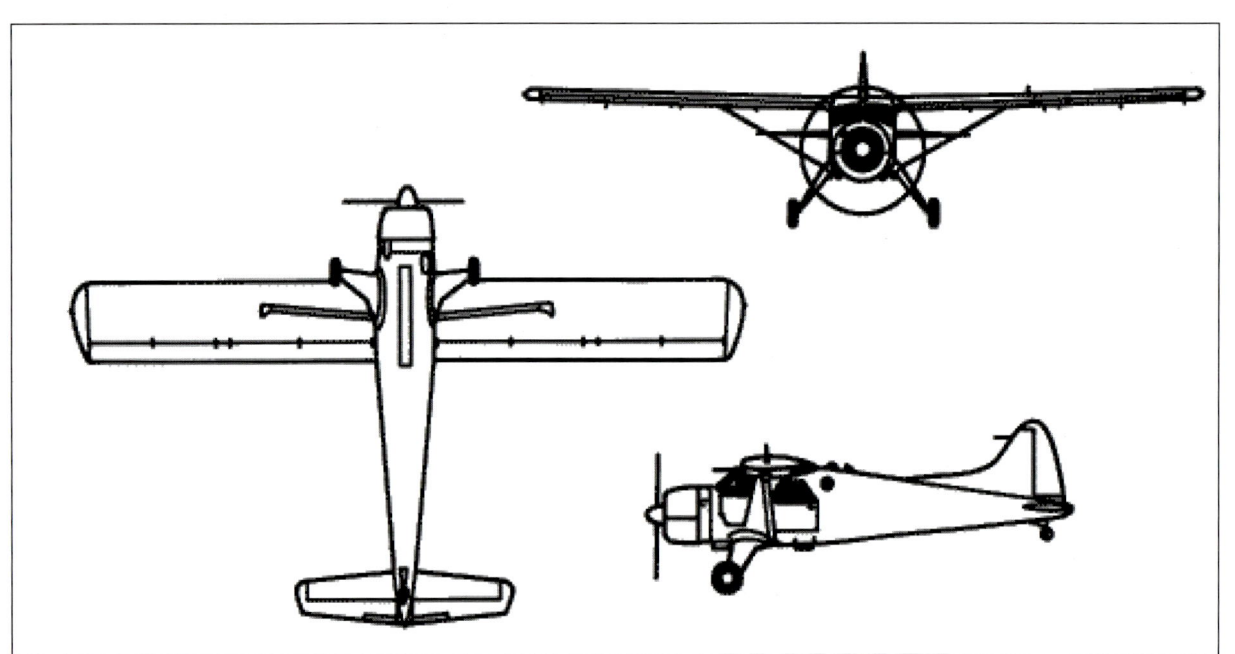

The RU-6A Beaver as depicted in an oil painting by Wayne Salge.

A dimensional representation of the U-6.

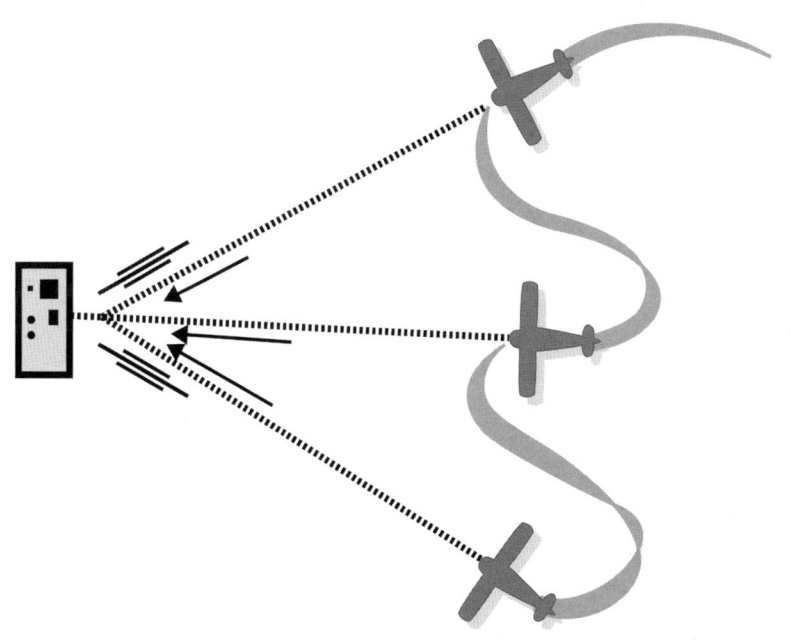

One of Hovey's early briefing diagrams depicting the ARDF process.

large areas and acquire precise coordinates, the 3d RRU deployed mobile direction-finding teams. Although the system of locating the transmitters worked well, the concept of operations suffered from the inherent delay in summoning troops to move on the reported locations. Far worse, encumbered with the heavy equipment of that day, deep in enemy territory, the small teams were vulnerable to ambush—and the Viet Cong was quick to exploit this weakness. In December 1961, an ambush killed ten members of a direction-finding team.

ASA commanders had to develop a new concept to avoid ambushes or face mission failure.[5] Engineers at ASA headquarters (Arlington Hall Station, Virginia) considered a number of options, including aerial platforms. With no answers at hand, engineers Herbert S. Hovey, Jr. (project leader), Charles Hawkins, and William Shade of the ASA Research and Development Agency (ASARDA) and EWL engineer Harold M. Jaffe traveled to Vietnam to study the signals environment.[6] Upon their return, joined by another EWL engineer John D. Woodward, the researchers concluded that the solution would have to come from the air.[7] Despite the obvious advantages of helicopters, experimentation proved they were ineffective due to excessive vibration.

With only the fixed-wing option left, the problem then revolved around finding an aircraft to accommodate direction-finding equipment.[8] The answer, although sophisticated, came in a simple package. ASA chose to develop an Army utility aircraft into its first ARDF platform. Designed as a "bush plane," the single-engine, high-wing, propeller-driven aircraft, originally called the de Havilland Canada DHC-2 Beaver proved an effective transport for remote areas around the world.[9] With its capability for

Hovey and Jaffe prepare the U-6 that would carry the first operational ARDF system in Vietnam.

short takeoff and landing and its rugged airframe, the Army recognized the Beaver's value as a utility transport in combat zones and purchased over seven hundred of them. Its subsequent military designation was U-6 (U stood for utility). The ubiquity of the U-6A version at U.S. military airfields in Vietnam guaranteed the availability of pilots, maintenance, and logistical support for the aircraft to any unit in the conflict. The SIGINT modified airplanes, redesignated as the RU-6A (R for reconnaissance), offered good visibility for the flight crew of two and had sufficient payload space for all necessary equipment along with room for a direction-finding operator.

The modifications required turning the aircraft itself into a giant direction finder by decoupling the antennae from its metal skin. Two dipole antennae were mounted above and below each wing, connected by twenty feet of cable to an R-390 radio receiver. With not much more equipment, the crew could map the origin of enemy stations. First, the direction-finding operator identified a transmission of importance. The pilot then pointed the aircraft in the direction of this transmission to achieve what they called a null signal. (A null signal could also be obtained by pointing the aircraft precisely in the opposite direction of the signal's origin.) The aircraft's wings had to be level with minimized rudder movement.

When the pilot was successful, the operator could take what they called a "shot" by noting the signal amplitude and determining a bearing. The pilot would then fly the airplane to different locations and repeat the process at least two more times. Once the crew had a minimum of three bearings, the operator or the copilot used them to triangulate the signal's location or fix. Fixes varied in accuracy from a few kilometers to less than one, depending on altitude, proximity to the target location, and the number of bearings taken. The collaborative effort between aviator and operator was the key to effectiveness.[10]

After successful ground testing, Hovey and Jaffe carried the equipment in their luggage via commercial flight to South Vietnam in March 1962. In the ensuing month, engineers and technicians worked out a way to install a C-12 compass, two Collins receivers, and two dipole antennae—one mounted on each wing. The system was then complete for test flights. Over the next two months, they worked out serious teething problems. The final product was three complete RU-6As, ready for operational flights. The results were nothing short of dramatic.

Herbert S. Hovey, Jr. began his service with ASA in 1958. Working mainly at Fort Monmouth and Vint Hill Farms Station, he spent thirty-three years developing infant technologies, such as ARDF and remotely controlled receiving systems, into functional equipment, ready for use in ASA and later INSCOM.

The first ARDF fix made in combat, occurring on 27 May 1962, vectored U.S. artillery onto a Viet Cong encampment, inflicting four-hundred enemy casualties.

For the first time, the Army could accurately pinpoint guerrilla forces in a timely manner. ARDF would be the reason why the 3d RRU was the first unit in Vietnam to receive the Army Meritorious Unit Commendation.[11] Moreover, the ARDF program continued to develop and expand. Reflecting on his career, Hovey remembered when he heard about the members lost in

The black cat of the 3d RRU was the first of many patches that ASA soldiers would wear to represent their aviation units worldwide.

To soldiers of the 3d RRU, Teeny Ween Airlines or TWA became its own brand.

ASA humor did not die with the expansion of the 3d RRU Aviation Section.

The tradition of wearing informal patches began in ASA when soldiers found they were unable to wear their official patch for reasons of security in sensitive locations. No image, however, was intended to replace the iconic and official ASA patch.

that ambushed direction-finding team on the ground and thinking that designers "owe it to them to give them the equipment with good performance to justify the risk they take."[12] Hovey went on to direct the continued development of ARDF and many other systems that advanced the Army's intelligence capabilities.

Although U.S. forces in Vietnam brought ARDF to what appeared in hindsight to be its inevitable conclusion, Hovey had his doubts at the time when two of his three initial test airframes failed to produce the desired results. His recollections of this puzzling occurrence were recorded in an interview, conducted by Dennis Buley in 1998:

> Initially, only one of the three aircraft functioned correctly. All were at a loss to understand why this was so. Only after much head scratching and tearing apart of the aircraft, was the problem identified. The two aircraft that did not function had been subjected to an IRAN (Inspect and Repair As Necessary) program and key mating surfaces between the wings, struts and fuselage had been painted. This caused decreased electrical conductivity, which, in turn, caused the ARDF system to malfunction. The aircraft that did function had not. Thus, it became necessary to select U-6A aircraft that had not been through the IRAN program…Suppose the test U-6A at Fort Monmouth had gone through the IRAN program? Would the Army's ARDF program have succeeded?[13]

An early version of the RU-8D configured with the CEFISH PERSON system for ARDF in Vietnam.

The 3d RRU's Aviation Section, established in June 1963, moved to capitalize on the success of ARDF through rapid expansion. Soldiers of the 3d RRU affectionately called Hovey's first three ARDF aircraft the TWA, which stood for "Teeny Weeny Airlines."[14] They were soon augmented by seven JU-6As—another variant of the U-6A—codenamed SEVEN ROSES. The potential for enhancement was far ranging. ASA's next move was the acquisition of new aircraft types, the first of which was the twin-engine, all-weather U-8 Seminole—a military derivation of the Beech Aircraft Corporation's D50B Twin Bonanza executive transport.

Searching for higher-performing aircraft, developers immediately recognized the value of the U-8D variant of the Seminole for ARDF. By the early 1960s, the Army had at least two hundred of these utility aircraft, formerly designated as the L-23 Seminole, mainly to transport staff officers and perform radar surveillance functions.[15] Entering service in Vietnam for the 3d RRU in 1963, the RU-8D, as it was redesignated for ASA missions, offered some significant advantages over the RU-6A Beaver. First, having space for five passengers, the Seminole had more room for navigational equipment. Second, the extra space allowed for a crew of four: pilot, co-pilot, mission plotter, and radio operator. Finally, in comparison to the RU-6A's performance, the RU-8D with twin engines

Positioned behind the RU-8D cockpit on the left is the operator's AN/ARD-15 Direction Finder, an essential part of the WINEBOTTLE system.

could operate in mountainous regions, reach higher altitudes, travel at greater speeds, achieve longer flight durations, and fly in "near all weather" conditions. The aircraft, however, lagged behind the RU-6A in the accuracy of fixes.

Within a year, the RU-8D would outnumber any other aerial platform serving in ASA's ARDF units, reaching a peak of forty-four in service by 1968, and subsequently earn the reputation for being the Army's airborne-SIGINT workhorse in Vietnam. With the adaptation of Doppler navigational radar on RU-8s, pilots flew at higher altitudes with extended ranges and relied less on visual recognition to determine their location.[16] As a new fleet of aerial platforms, RU-8Ds, along with RU-6As, carried mission gear known by the nicknames CHECKMATE, WINEBOTTLE, and CEFISH PERSON.

An operator prepares equipment in the RU-8D.

RU-8D patches

The RU-8D Seminole became the ASA's workhorse for ARDF in Vietnam.

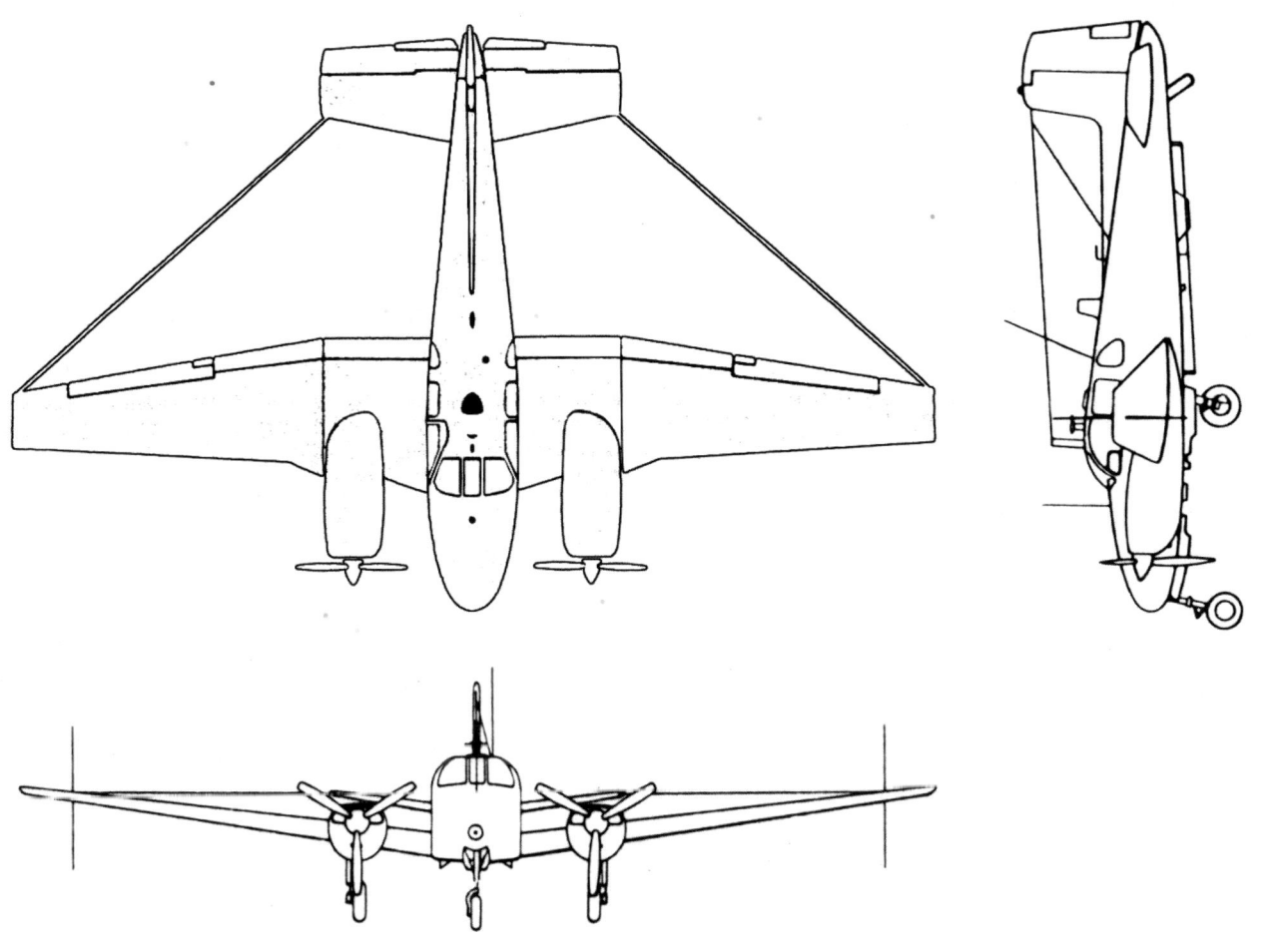

A dimensional representation of the RU-8D.

MG McChristian, the J2, MACV, with his staff.

A Deeper Commitment

In 1964, Vietnam was proving a formidable challenge for the Army. Following the insertion of large numbers of American troops after the Gulf of Tonkin incident, the U.S. military role in South Vietnam grew from an advisory status to full assistance. By 1965, the Military Assistance Command-Vietnam (MACV), the joint command entity for American forces in-country, received intelligence from a variety of sources. Its J2, Major General Joseph A. McChristian, headed the 525th Military Intelligence Group, which functioned as a staff headquarters as well as an operational unit.

The 1st MIBARS served in Vietnam as the primary Army unit for imagery interpretation from 1965 to 1972. Photographic Specialist Robert Bills stands in front of the 1st MIBARS Imagery Interpretation Section at Phu Bai.

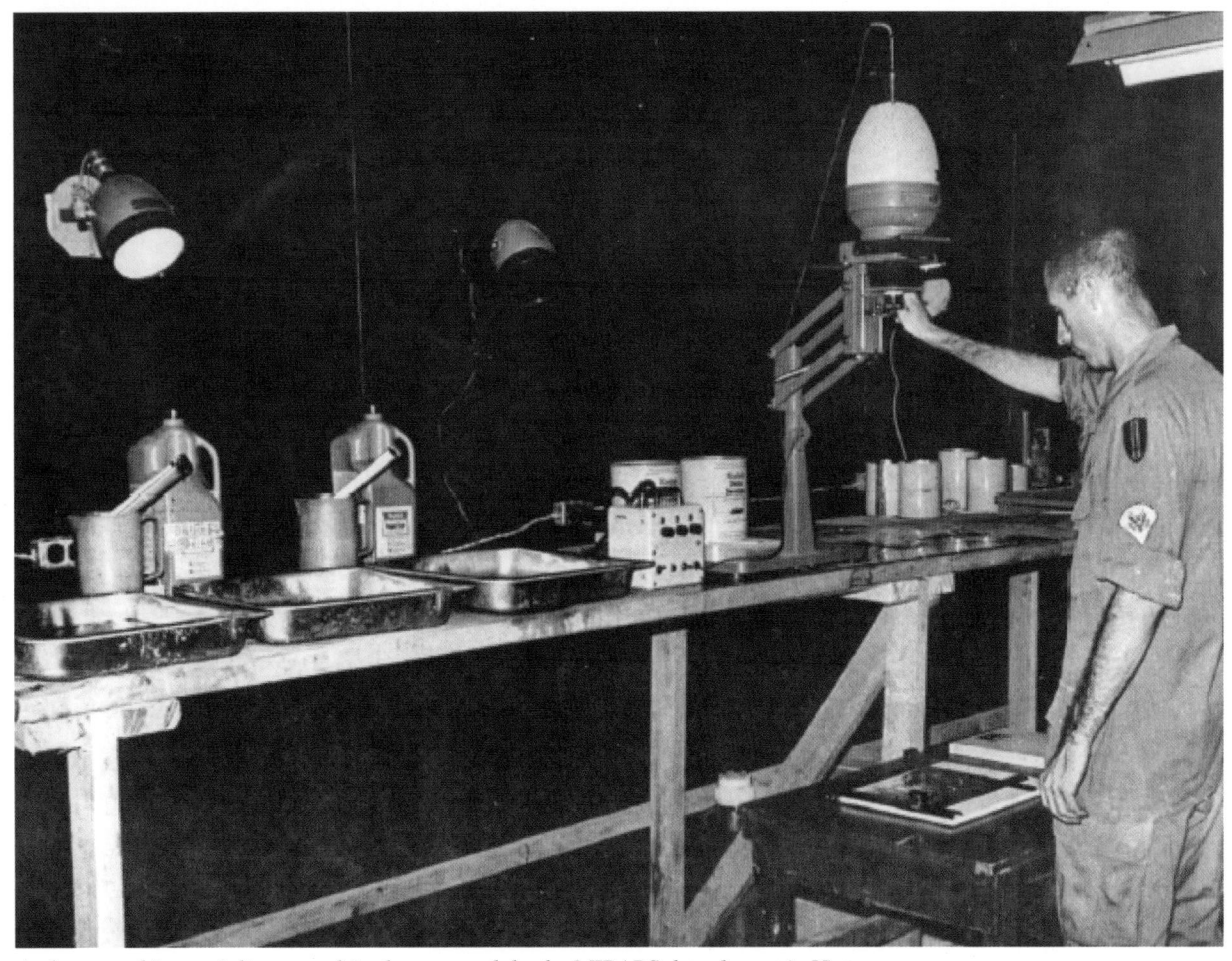

A photographic specialist at work in the camera lab of a MIBARS detachment in Vietnam.

Among the group's diverse assortment of six battalions was the 1st Military Intelligence Battalion (Air Reconnaissance Support) (Field Army), better known as the 1st MIBARS.[17] Formerly the 1st Air Reconnaissance Battalion, the unit was converted and redesignated on 20 March 1962 for MI assignment. On 23 December 1965, its headquarters moved from Fort Bragg, North Carolina, to Saigon, South Vietnam. Support missions included processing, interpreting, annotating, reproducing, and delivering airborne imagery and visual sightings obtained from tactical Army and Air Force reconnaissance elements. The U.S. Air Force Tactical Reconnaissance Program was the battalion's main provider of collection. As other duties, the unit managed air-reconnaissance liaison officers and disseminated its collected information that directly supported the Army in Vietnam.

The Air Force, observing the Army's successes, also produced its own ARDF platforms. Together, the two services employed more than 130 aircraft in this effort and tacitly established

Army and Air Force personnel in the ARDF Coordination Center (ACC) reported directly to the J2, MACV.

lines of mission demarcation. The Air Force ARDF systems normally flew reconnaissance missions at higher altitudes, while the Army flew in the lower to medium altitudes, targeting fixes of smaller radius (300 to 500 meters) for artillery support fire.[18] The resulting data from ASA aircraft were generally more useful to Army tactical units. On 1 July 1966, MACV authorized the jointly manned ARDF Coordination Center (ACC) under the supervision of the newly formed 509th Radio Research (RR) Group, which replaced the 3d RRU. Staffed by personnel from the 509th RR Group and the Air Force's 6994th Security Squadron, the ACC tasked all ARDF assets, evaluated incoming data, and reported analysis to MACV. This arrangement streamlined organization, reduced redundancy, and optimized the ARDF effort in South Vietnam.

The main gate of Davis Station, headquarters of the 509th RR Group.

As U.S. forces in Vietnam steadily grew to unprecedented levels, MACV leaned on ARDF to plan attacks. Its systems could fly over a vast territory, which was inaccessible to other collection methods, and the ACC could redirect their efforts on short notice. In response to MACV's demand for more surveillance of targets in the field, ASA produced a consistent flow of intelligence about Marxist infiltration units operating in the South through a combined analysis of traffic and direction-finding data collected by many aircraft flying at low altitudes over suspected enemy

An aerial view of the 3d RRU headquarters building, located at Tan Son Nhut Air Base, Saigon.
The location later became the headquarters of the 224th Aviation Battalion (at position 4).
The headquarters of the 509th RR Group was across the street (at position 1).

positions. The numerous SIGINT successes, attributable to ARDF, made it a highly visible asset for command support and sponsorship from technical sectors of both the government and industry.

As the war escalated in the latter part of 1965, MACV requested more aircraft and crews only to realize that any increase was never enough. By year's end, ASA had thirty ARDF platforms at its disposal. The success of ground operations supported by airborne SIGINT convinced the Joint Chiefs of Staff and the Department of the Army to procure forty-one aerial platforms for a concerted ARDF effort, which involved expanding Project WINEBOTTLE. Meanwhile, the MACV commander, General William C. Westmoreland, decided to place ARDF resources on priority for close tactical support missions.[19]

The next phase of this expansion involved the development of a new system of command and control. In the early years of the conflict, ASA had a relatively simple structure in South Vietnam with two detachments of the former 3d RRU responsible for all ARDF. By mid-1965, the Army had a substantially larger presence in-country. Its forces were now divided into four tactical zones, each charged to counter threats from North Vietnam as well as domestic insurgency. Subsequently, the ASA leadership planned a comprehensive restructuring in kind to resolve operational and administrative disparities and to accommodate the growth of ARDF.

ASA moved its aerial assets (having grown to two detachments) under the command of a newly created unit, the 224th Aviation Battalion (Radio Research), effective 1 June 1966 and concurrent with the establishment of the 509th RR Group—the battalion's higher headquarters. The battalion would have four companies: the 138th Aviation Company (Radio Research) at Da Nang and Phu Bai in support of the I Corps Tactical Zone; the 144th Aviation Company (Radio Research) with platoons at An Khe and Holloway Army Airfield, Pleiku, in support of the II Corps Tactical Zone; the 146th Aviation Company (Radio Research) at Tan Son Nhut Air Base, Saigon, in support of the III Corps Tactical Zone; and the 156th Aviation Company (Radio Research) at Can Tho in support of the IV Corps Tactical Zone. On 3 July 1967, the 1st Radio Research Company (Aviation) was assigned to the 224th Aviation Battalion as a direct support unit for MACV instead of a corps tactical zone. All ASA fixed-wing assets were assigned to these five companies.[20]

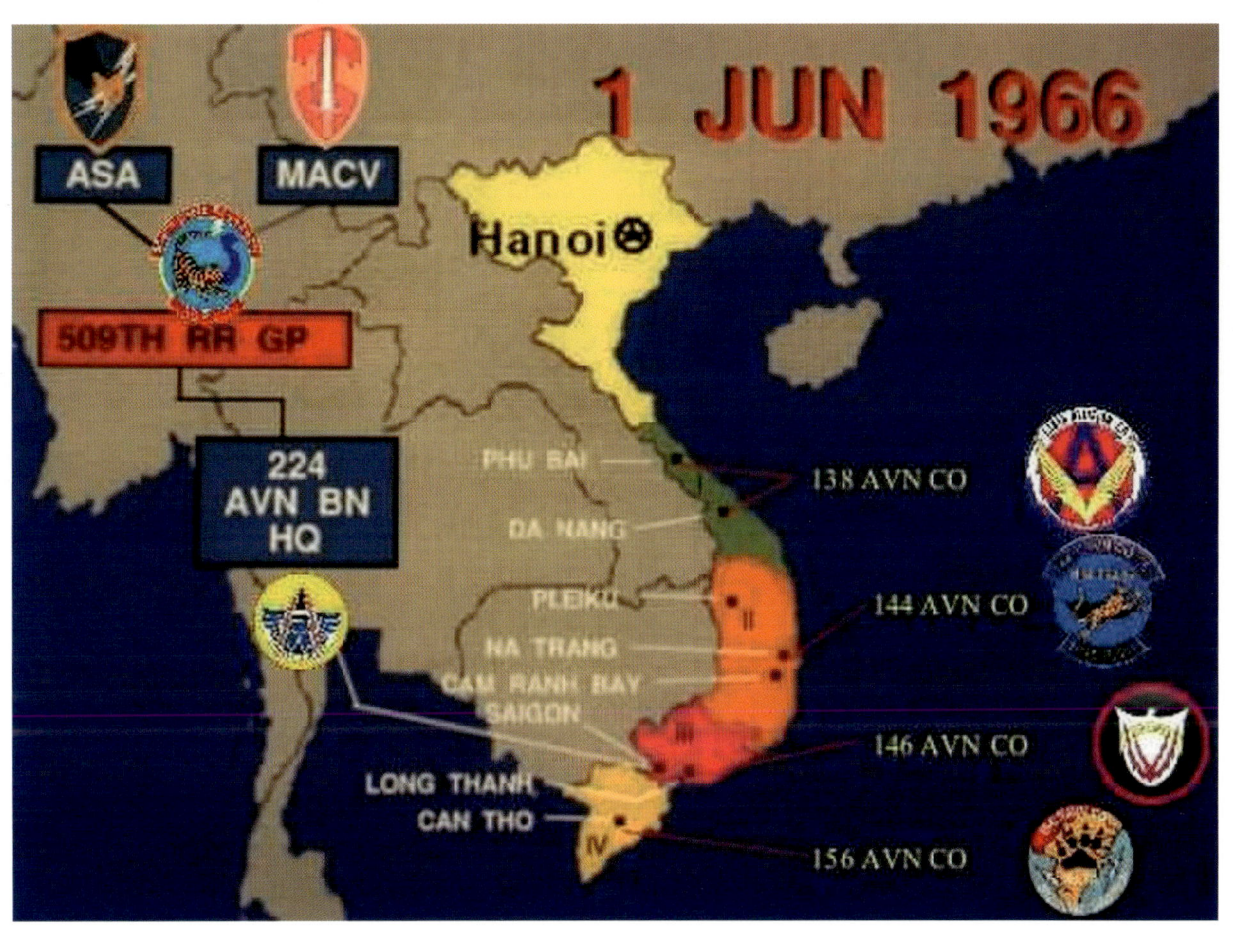

1 JUN 1966

The command and staff officers of the 224th Aviation Battalion in August 1966. LTC Richard A. Rusk (fourth from left) was the first permanent battalion commander.

The 224th Aviation Battalion started with thirty-six aircraft and 169 soldiers. At first the unit was assigned a new call sign every week, but after a number of misunderstandings with air traffic control, the random generation of call signs was abandoned. The last one generated, "Lonely Ringer," became permanent and stuck with the battalion henceforth as its nickname. In succeeding years, MACV would depend on this aviation unit, ultimately increasing its strength to eighty aircraft and 1,066 soldiers.[21] The decision to invest in a battalion-sized structure paid off not only by encompassing the growing number of men and equipment but also by elevating an important mission out of obscurity as strategic planners sometimes erroneously associate mission importance with unit size. Peaking in June 1969, then gradually downsizing toward

COL W. Riley, Commander of the 509th RR Group, watches as COL Thompson of MACV attaches the Meritorious Unit Citation Banner to the 224th Aviation Battalion colors (March 1968).

Not only seen on patches and the unit colors, the "Lonely Ringer" symbol was ubiquitous throughout the battalion.

inactivation on 3 March 1973, the Lonely Ringer had participated in fifteen campaigns and received three Army Meritorious Unit Commendations and the Republic of Vietnam Cross of Gallantry with Palm.[22]

Among its three aerial-intelligence missions—ARDF, communications intercept, and electronic jamming—90 percent of the battalion's assets were devoted to ARDF. By the middle of 1968, the unit was contributing four-thousand fixes per month to ground commands. The majority of fixes received conventional countermeasures such as artillery fire and air strikes. When senior officers held their fire on fixes to safeguard their intelligence source, the information remained consequential as a warning mechanism to protect fire support bases and isolated outposts. During one mission, for instance, an ARDF platform reported a fix in front of an advancing convoy. The ensuing warning from the ACC allowed the convoy commander to circumvent a Viet Cong ambush.

It was unusual for aircrews to witness an action against a target that they located. In this rare case, Operator Clark Sullins photographs a B-52 airstrike against a recently acquired ARDF target.

Flying an aircraft for the 224th Aviation Battalion was an unusual mission for the Army and ASA. "Radio research" was a shallow cover story. Pilots and crew wore patches of the signal corps on their shoulders in lieu of the ASA eagle. At a meeting with the entire unit in attendance, battalion commander Lieutenant Colonel Robert Swanson asked if the "real signal officer" would come forward. As expected, only one soldier, a lieutenant in the signal branch, stepped up to be recognized. Battalion personnel rarely knew what became of the intelligence that they collected. After a flight, information went to the ACC and the field stations for further analysis and then to MACV. On occasion, a crew might observe an airstrike or an artillery barrage on a previously identified location, but more often than not, they flew only on the assurance that MACV needed a reliable intelligence picture.

MACV wanted ARDF platforms in the air as much as possible. ARDF missions flew in daylight hours because the enemy transmitted most of his messages before dark and navigational orientation often depended on observable checkpoints. Aircraft typically took off just before dawn. After a four-hour mission, pilots and operators went on with other duties throughout the day. In the meantime, other missions went up. In a surge, aircraft only landed to refuel and change crews. During the Lam Son 719 offensive by U.S. and South Vietnamese forces in 1971, for instance, the skies were crowded with ARDF assets of all types, in support of ground operations. Flight surgeons were also busy at these times as pilots were required to have an examination after thirty consecutive days of flight. Although maintenance was Swanson's most pressing problem, weather conditions and fuel supply were most often the determinant factors for down time.

Rookie operators in the back of the aircraft often suffered air sickness. Having to sit perpendicular to the direction of flight while the pilots performed complex maneuvers to get a fix, they sacrificed their breakfast or lunch for the mission. Air sickness was especially difficult for Vietnamese linguists who had no previous flying experience.[23]

There were constant reminders of danger on almost every flight. Missions were flown sanitized, which meant nobody on an aircraft brought his wallet, pictures, or personal items. Instead, aircrews were issued "blood chits"—a piece of cloth with a bounty written in several languages, including Chinese and Russian, offering a handsome reward for the safe return of the downed aviator or operator. In addition, each soldier had a weapon. Officers carried .38-caliber revolvers, and enlisted were armed with M-16 rifles or .45-caliber pistols. Battalion personnel sometimes joked that they only needed two bullets if they survived a crash: one to suppress the enemy advancement and the other to put themselves out of their misery. Nevertheless, all flyers had plenty of ammunition, and protecting the cryptologic gear was all important. When an aircraft went down in unfriendly territory, soldiers risked their lives to deny sensitive equipment and material to the enemy.

Aviators had to be watchful. Shortly after takeoff, the copilot had to check "the gun target line" with the field artillery net to ensure that his flight path did not intersect with shelling from friendly artillery units and battleships offshore or with air strikes from B-52s and aircraft carrier-based bombers. It was also important to monitor air command and control nets for advisories of North Vietnamese interceptor aircraft in the area.

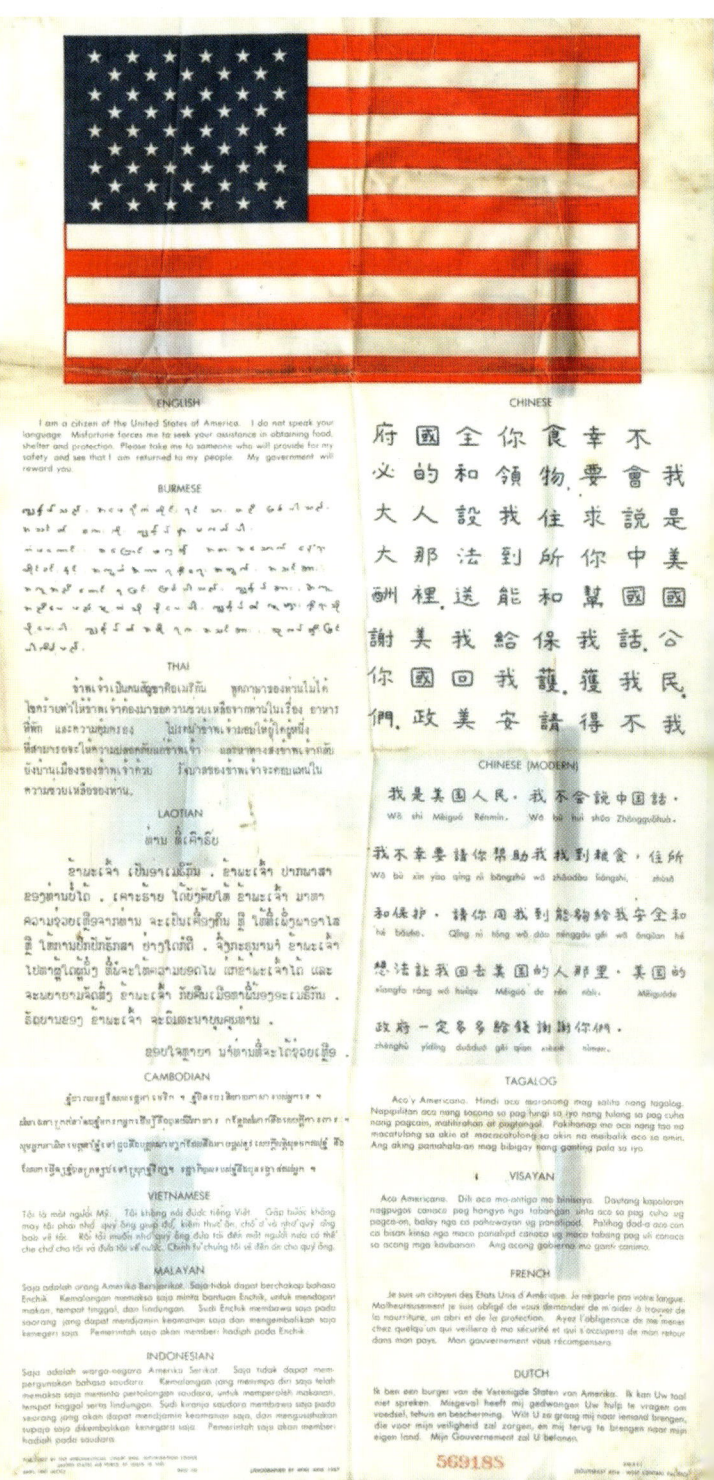

The escapee translation cloth was commonly known as the "blood chit" among soldiers of the 224th Aviation Battalion.

Navigation difficulties might have been the most critical problem. Pilots relied on navigational aids called tactical air navigation systems (TACANS) that sometimes malfunctioned or were destroyed by enemy fire. Without them, the crew hoped that an outdated map and a compass would see them through. It was not unusual for a pilot to have stories about being lost deep in enemy territory and having to fly to the coast for safety. He would not dare backtrack; the North Vietnamese would certainly be awaiting his return.

Aircrews of the 1st RR Company check flight gear in front of their RP-2E CRAZY CAT aircraft.

The 1st Radio Research Company

Among the Lonely Ringer's units, the 1st Radio Research Company was unique in its overall mission. Activated in December 1966, it was organized as the 1st Army Security Agency Company (Aviation) at Fort Devens, Massachusetts, where its personnel trained before going to Cam Ranh Bay on 1 July 1967. Supporting only MACV directly and having the designation 1st Radio Research (RR) Company while in Vietnam, the unit flew collection missions with specialized equipment.

It was the only unit to use the P-2V Neptune, a Navy four-engine aircraft and the largest in ASA's Vietnam air fleet. The Army requested five of these aerial platforms to carry the CRAZY CAT (later renamed CEFLIEN LION) system—the largest and heaviest of airborne-SIGINT payloads. Piloted by Army aviators, the Neptune accommodated thirteen operator positions, a quantity unsurpassed in MI aviation. The modified aircraft was redesignated as the RP-2E. According to specifications, these aircraft were capable of flying on station for fourteen hours, and in one case, an RP-2E sustained a flight exceeding seventeen hours.

The RP-2E was a modified version of the Lockheed P-2V Neptune, flown by the U.S. Navy.

CRAZY CAT (CEFLIEN LION) systems inside the RP-2E.

Revetment area of the 1st RR Company, Cam Rahn Bay, Vietnam. Three RP-2E CRAZY CAT (CEFLIEN LION) aircraft are parked while an RU-8D WINEBOTTLE leaves for takeoff (June 1970).

An early version of a 1st RR Company patch depicting the CRAZY CAT system.

Later version of a 1st RR Company patch when its main system was known as CEFLIEN LION.

Soldiers of the 156th Aviation Company in formation.

CEFLIEN LION provided an onboard EW capability with five AN/MLQ-29 countermeasure systems; however, its jamming potential was rarely if ever used. Its true value came as a SIGINT collector.[24] The system could gather COMINT in both very-high-frequency (VHF) and HF mode. It proved most effective at targeting the voice traffic from the General Directorate Rear Services of North Vietnam, the supervisory authority of movement and infiltration of enemy personnel, supplies, and equipment into South Vietnam. The Army had no other system that could match the volume of production from CEFLIEN LION. In fact, only the expense of its logistical requirements matched its prolific output. Consequently, the 1st RR Company also had RU-8Ds in its inventory to operate WINEBOTTLE systems as a measure to economize on missions of lesser duration. MACV was using CEFLIEN LION up until one month before the 1st RR Company was inactivated on 30 April 1972.[25] The 1st RR Company received two Army Meritorious Unit Commendations and the Republic of Vietnam Cross of Gallantry with Palm.[26]

The 156th Aviation Company (Radio Research)

The 156th Aviation Company (Radio Research) had the fewest airborne systems, five RU-6As and one RU-8D. Nevertheless, its crews still managed thousands of sorties.[27] In June 1968, the unit added a single OV-1C Mohawk with direction-finding gear, nicknamed HOMING PIGEON. Its equipment proved ineffective and was withdrawn from service three months later.

The underside of a tiger paw became a common representation on patches of the 156th Aviation Company.

While in-country, the 156th Aviation Company won three Army Meritorious Unit Commendations and the Republic of Vietnam Cross of Gallantry with Palm.[28] These accolades, however, did not come without sacrifice. On 24 November 1970, an RU-6A collided with a UH-1H helicopter, southeast of Can Tho Airfield. Chief Warrant Officer 2 Robert D. Perry, Chief Warrant Officer 2 Warren H. Mobley, and Specialist 6 Norman F. Evans were unit fatalities. On 27 April 1972, ASA reduced the company to zero strength and transferred its colors to Biggs Army Airfield, Fort Bliss, Texas.[29]

HOMING PIDGEON was a one-of-kind ARDF system on the OV-1C Mohawk aerial platform.

The flight line of the 146th Aviation Company at Long Thanh.

The 146th Aviation Company (Radio Research)

The 146th Aviation Company (Radio Research) started with six RU-6As and seven RU-8Ds but quickly expanded its aerial-system inventory from the output of ASA's developmental branch in the United States. A few months after the unit's activation on 1 June 1966, it picked up the RCV-2B— a de Havilland Canada Caribou—as an aerial platform for a system nicknamed PATHFINDER. Its service lasted less than a year, ending when an Air Force initiative removed all Caribous from Army service. In March 1967, the first of three RU-1A Otters arrived to function as an aerial platform for CAFÉ GIRL (originally called HAPPY NIGHTS)—an ARDF system with a manual Morse-code frequency finder. The RU-1A was a modified de Havilland Canada (DHC) Otter—a single-engine, high-wing, propeller-driven, short-takeoff-and-landing-capable aircraft.[30] For all intents and purposes, the Otter was a larger version of the DHC-2 (or U-6) Beaver, both aircraft being well-suited for bush pilots in Northern Canada and Alaska. Appreciating its potential as a light tactical aircraft, the Army adapted it (designated as the U-1A) to be a transport capable of carrying large payloads into inhospitable locations.

Nicknamed "Snoopers," soldiers of the 146th Aviation Company stand at ease during an award ceremony (December 1966).

PATHFINDER on the DeHavilland Caribou RCV-2B aerial platform. The mission crew would never forget the day when a North Vietnamese 37mm antiaircraft round pierced the vertical stabilizer and .30 caliber rounds hit the fuselage. Fortunately for them, the aircraft landed safely without any casualties.

As displayed on the cowling, a Snoopy character was the unofficial mascot of the 146th Aviation Company. After a long morning mission, crews were typically welcomed by the midday heat upon landing.

The 146th Aviation Company's patches give visual representation to the unit's nickname.

ASA later acquired and converted another RU-1A for project SORE THUMB, which employed a spinning adcock array antenna—capable of 360-degree VHF direction finding—in flight. The project proved less than successful for field use, but later improvements on the antenna led to the development of the more successful LEFT JAB system.

CAFÉ GIRL, going beyond ARDF, was ASA's second successful attempt at airborne collection. The aircraft carried one operator, but a later reconfiguration allowed for two. In December 1967, ASA sent two more RU-1As to the 146th Aviation Company with upgraded systems, called LAFFING OTTER. Unlike the systems on the RU-8D and the RU-6A, CAFÉ GIRL and LAFFING OTTER were able to perform single-aircraft direction finding at lower frequencies and collect signals for analysis. These systems remained in service until January 1971.

On 12 February 1969, a large caliber antiaircraft round hit the underside of an RU-1A LAFFING OTTER over Tay Ninh, South Vietnam, near the Cambodian border. The pilot, Major Querin Herlick, managed to crash land the aircraft in a rice paddy 1.5 miles into Cambodia. The occupants, two aviators and two operators, all of whom survived, managed to destroy all sensitive material and equipment while delaying the Viet Cong with suppressive fire. The capture of the four soldiers

RU-1A, carrying the LAFFING OTTER system, provided ASA with a more affordable alternative to the RP-2E CRAZY CAT as an aerial collection platform in Vietnam.

led to a three-month detainment by the North Vietnamese until the Cambodian government secured their repatriation.[31]

In an effort to expand the dual role of collection and ARDF, ASA introduced yet more of the latest equipment to the 146th Aviation Company. One new system, called LAFFING EAGLE, was integrated with a U-21D aircraft. Through the 1960s, the Army had purchased a large number of Beechcraft Model 90 series King Airs from the Beech Aircraft Corporation to use as utility aircraft, designated as the U-21 Ute.[32] The reconnaissance variant was called the RU-21D, the last of ASA's aircraft acquisitions for service in Vietnam. Established as the standard foundation aerial platform, these aircraft would become the carriers for the most technologically advanced airborne-SIGINT

An RU-21D LAFFING EAGLE arrives in Vietnam.

systems in Vietnam and represented the future of ASA's aerial-intelligence programs for many years to come.

Having turboprop twin engines, the RU-21 was a step up from the RU-8D. As ARDF systems became larger and more sophisticated, ASA needed larger and more powerful aerial platforms. The RU-21 had a much greater range, speed, rate of climb, and payload capacity in comparison to any other ARDF platform previously in service. The cabin had room for three operators, an improved inertial navigation system, and receivers with greater frequency coverage. On 8 December 1968, the first sixteen RU-21Ds, using the LAFFING EAGLE system, were distributed among the 138th, 144th, and 146th Aviation Companies.

The first RU-21Ds entered service in December 1968.

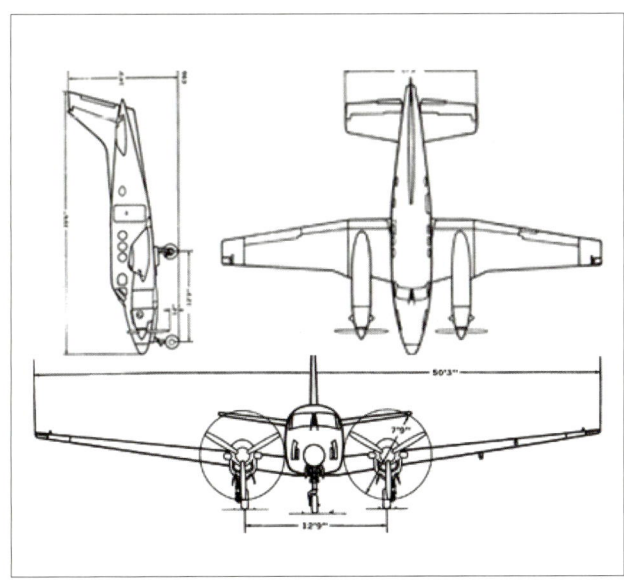

A dimensional representation of the RU-21D.

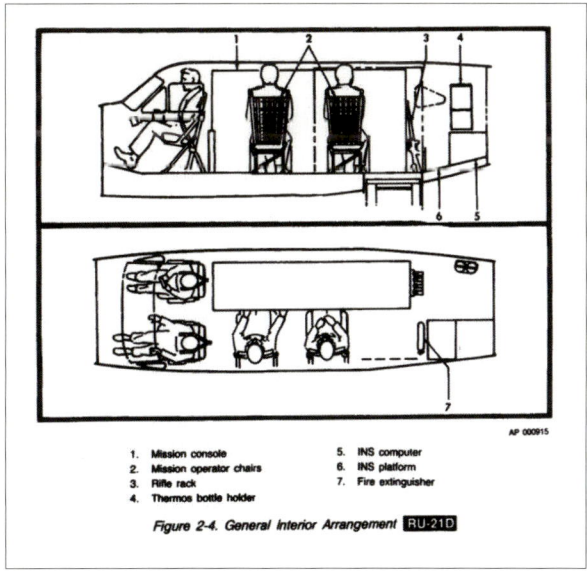

1. Mission console
2. Mission operator chairs
3. Rifle rack
4. Thermos bottle holder
5. INS computer
6. INS platform
7. Fire extinguisher

Figure 2-4. General Interior Arrangement RU-21D

A diagram of the interior arrangement of aviator and operator stations inside the RU-21D.

An operator's position inside the RU-21D.

LAFFING EAGLE had the ability to record low-level voice intercepts on tape, while the aircraft was engaged in ARDF. On the ground, a courier delivered the finished tapes to collection authorities. The flexibility of this system proved invaluable when it intercepted plans of the North Vietnamese Army 1st Division for an attack on 22 February 1969—the launch date of the second Tet Offensive—and located enemy voice transmitters in the southern delta and hill country. The installation of the AN/ARD-23 V-Scan on LAFFING EAGLE in October 1970 proved a major milestone in ARDF with its increased speed in recording fixes, ability to cover larger areas, and more accurate navigational system. Technologically, it kept Army airborne SIGINT in Vietnam on an equal footing with that of the Air Force. In 1972, the 146th Aviation Company transferred its RU-21Ds to the 138th Aviation Company, thereby simplifying maintenance logistics.

Later versions of the RU-21D LAFFING EAGLE in Vietnam had a civilian paint scheme.

Operating equipment and console of the LAFFING EAGLE system before installation in the RU-21D.

66

One of the more surprising challenges for the 146th Aviation Company and the headquarters of the 224th Aviation Battalion was their tenant status on Tan Son Nhut Air Base. The Air Force base commanders lacked an understanding of the battalion's mission and made little effort to accommodate its requirements. One incident in 1969 highlighted this problem. An Air Force security officer, obeying a standing curfew, denied a flight crew of the 146th Aviation Company access to its aircraft in the early morning hours. The urgency of the mission, however, compelled the captain in charge of the crew to ignore the Air Force officer's prohibitions and continue to his aircraft. Within the hour, Air Force security personnel arrived to arrest the captain, but found themselves at a standoff with ASA guards on the flight line, all with loaded firearms aimed at each other. The Air Force lieutenant in charge, observing that his men were outgunned and staring directly at the captain's .38-caliber pistol in the firing position, decided to stand down and resolve the misunderstanding upon the flight crew's return. As a result of this incident and a few less dramatic ones, the base commander granted an exception to the curfew for the 146th Aviation Company.

Not long after the standoff, on 5 June 1970, the company along with the 224th Aviation Battalion headquarters relocated to an Army airfield at Long Thanh where operations continued for three more years.[33][†] Prior to its inactivation on 17 February 1973 as part of the drawdown, the 146th Aviation Company was awarded three Army Meritorious Unit Commendations and the Republic of Vietnam Cross of Gallantry with Palm.[34]

† As a pilot in the 146th Aviation Company, Warrant Officer John B. Hyde was tasked to assess the South Vietnamese Air Force (VNAF) pilots who would fly RU-6A aircraft on ARDF missions in support of South Vietnamese forces. His findings determined that "VNAF pilots were highly competent in the aircraft and the mission, limited only by equipment/political problems."

Senior NCOs of the 144th Aviation Company.

The 144th Aviation Company (Radio Research)

The 144th Aviation Company (Radio Research) operated RU-8D and RU-21D aircraft in support of the I Field Force within the II Corps Tactical Zone. The company supported units that rotated in and out of the zone, including the 1st Cavalry Division (Air Mobile), 173d Airborne Brigade, 4th Infantry Division, 101st Airborne Division, Korean White Horse Division, and various special-forces units. During its service, the 144th Aviation Company won three Army Meritorious Unit Commendations and the Republic of Vietnam Cross of Gallantry with Palm.[35] As part of the drawdown in Vietnam, the company stood down in April 1971 and was officially inactivated on 30 September 1971.[36] The 138th Aviation Company assumed its mission and authority over its remaining personnel.[37]

The flight-line operations center of the 144th Aviation Company at Nha Trang.

The fight line of the 144th Aviation Company at Nha Trang.

WO Redding of the 144th Aviation Company reviews his preflight checklist before takeoff.

Patches of the 144th Aviation Company.

The 138th Aviation Company (Radio Research)

Activated at Da Nang on 1 June 1966, the 138th Aviation Company (Radio Research) was the first of the 224th Aviation Battalion's companies. It started with systems using RU-8Ds and later received RU-21D LAFFING EAGLEs and JU-21A LEFT JABs—the most sophisticated of the Army ARDF systems.

The I Corps Tactical Zone was the farthest north and the most dangerous area of Vietnam, which included the A Shau Valley, Quang Tri, Da Nang, and Chu Lai, as well as areas where a pilot could easily fly into North Vietnam or Laos due to the slightest miscalculation. Consequently, the 138th Aviation Company suffered the heaviest losses within the 224th Aviation Battalion. On 15 November 1966, an RU-6A went missing while on a ferry flight from Dong Ha to Da Nang; Captain Harry M. Ravenna was not seen again. On 4 December 1967, an RU-8D crashed. The fatalities were Captain J. O. Douglas Kelly and Warrant Officer 1 Robert D. King. On 29 December 1967, another RU-8D crashed. This time, it was on takeoff from Da Nang killing Warrant Officer 1 Milton W. Smith and Warrant Officer 1 Jonathan P. Shaffer. Specialist 4 Jose L. Lujan was mortally wounded.[38]

Soldiers of the 138th Aviation Company in formation.

The flight line of the 138th Aviation Company at Da Nang.

Members of the 138th Aviation Company work on an RU-8D. Visible on the engine cowling, the "Pink Panther" was the unofficial symbol of the 138th Aviation Company.

Patches of the 138th Aviation Company.

SP5 Clark Sullins

The highest death toll from an incident occurred on 4 March 1971 when a JU-21A LEFT JAB, call sign Vanguard 216, was shot down, most likely by a surface-to-air missile. The crew of Vanguard 216 perished, but their names are not forgotten: Captain Michael Marker, Warrant Officer 1 Harold Algaard, Specialist 6 John Strawn, Specialist 5 Richard Jay, and Specialist 5 Rodney Osborne.[39] After the tragic loss of Vanguard 216, all of the maintenance and training difficulties seemed insignificant for the soldiers in the 138th Aviation Company. Captain Marker and his crew were not only pilots, trainers, and operators but also comrades, who died in the line of duty, serving in a cohesive unit.

Although North Vietnam was off limits to ARDF missions, there were times when the mass movement of North Vietnamese forces into South Vietnam necessitated flights over enemy territory. As it was, ARDF missions in the I Corps Tactical Zone were prone to navigation problems, which resulted in inadvertent collection opportunities over North Vietnam. In other cases, however, volunteers flew over the border to guard against suspected surprise offensives.

On one occasion, during the Easter Offensive of 1972, ASA's 8th Radio Research Field Station at Phu Bai had determined that the 324B Division of the North Vietnamese Army was moving south along the coast into South Vietnam. When the information reached George Jacks, a senior direction-finding operator and ASA noncommissioned officer, at the field station, he contacted an associate ASA operator in the 138th Aviation Company, Specialist 5 Clark Sullins, and proposed an unorthodox mission over North Vietnam. Obtaining tacit permission from the company commander, Jacks and Sullins, along with two volunteer aviators, flew missions in an RU-21D LAFFING EAGLE system over the 324B Division's staging area for three consecutive days. Not long after the last ARDF mission, B-52 bombers began flying sorties over the resulting targets. The 324B Division suffered six-hundred casualties, shattering its fighting capacity in South Vietnamese territory.[40]

Partly due to its proximity to the North Vietnamese border, the 138th Aviation Company became a cohesive unit that could play as hard as it worked. On Christmas Eve, for example, the company officers regularly substituted for the enlisted men on guard duty. On other occasions, unit cohesion could take other forms. At their base on the grounds of the 8th Radio Research Field Station in Phu Bai, the soldiers chose the movie image of the Pink Panther as their company

View of the runway at Da Nang on a standard approach.

mascot. Navy and Marine personnel who shared the base were often taken by surprise when they discovered that certain items of naval property, such as the large anchor on display at the front gate, had changed color overnight from grey to pink. In spite of the occasional prank, the Navy demonstrated its appreciation by awarding the 138th Aviation Company a Navy Meritorious Unit Commendation for support to the III Marine Amphibious Force from May 1967 to July 1969.[41] The unit's decorations also included two Army Meritorious Unit Commendations and the Republic of Vietnam Cross of Gallantry with Palm.[42] The 138th Aviation Company was the last unit of the Lonely Ringer to remain on duty, inactivating on 1 March 1973, when U.S. forces completed their drawdown.[43]

A JU-21A in flight provides a clear representation of LEFT JAB's distinctive radome in full extension.

LEFT JAB

Next to CRAZY CAT/CEFLIEN LION, the three LEFT JAB AN/ARQ-28 systems used by the 138th Aviation Company represented the culmination of airborne-SIGINT advancement in Vietnam. The system was implemented as a "package concept" undergoing the testing of equipment and training of operators before going into combat, which led to the smoothest deployment of an ASA airborne system in Vietnam. Three of these aircraft arrived in Vietnam on 5 December 1970 and became operational on 9 January 1971. LEFT JAB, like LAFFING EAGLE, used the U-21 platform, redesignated as the JU-21A. Unlike most RU-21s and all other ARDF aircraft, the JU-21A had a civilian paint scheme with no camouflage and was equipped with the AN/APR-39 Radar Warning Device to avoid antiaircraft fire.[44]

The system provided 360-degree direction-finding coverage of radio frequencies (including VHF) by extending a rotating "spaced loop" antenna from the underside of the aircraft after takeoff. Instead of maneuvering the airplane to a null signal, the spinning loop inside a radome would detect the null during its rotation. The pilot only had to fly on a specific arc to learn the direction of a target. This method eliminated the need to move from one checkpoint to another, the most time-consuming part of ARDF. A digital computer stored direction-finding data and determined the aircraft's position. Its secure voice radio and audio intercom system facilitated communications among operators, pilots, and field stations. These advances not only augmented the number of fixes per mission but also reduced stress on the airframe. Even so, training had to be intensive to inculcate aviators in the complexities of this new technology.

Assigned to the 138th Aviation Company to monitor the demilitarized zone (DMZ) between North and South Vietnam, the systems were an immediate success and in high demand. The commanding general of the 1st Brigade, 5th Infantry Division, expressed his appreciation for LEFT JAB: "I would like to have LEFT JAB over my area of operation 24 hours per day..."[45] On one occasion, MACV wanted LEFT JAB in the air, flying an additional duty, to provide force protection for comedian Bob Hope's USO Show. At another time, the commanding general of the 101st Airborne Division wanted to task LEFT JAB with locating a practical joker who was playing music on his command net. For this particular request, MACV agreed with the leader of the 138th Aviation Company's operations platoon to deny the general. As a result of a heavy workload, the 138th Aviation Company had to initiate an in-country training program for its pilots and maintenance personnel to shorten LEFT JAB's downtime.

As a cutting-edge technology, the aircraft's unique capabilities sometimes posed unique problems. For maintenance personnel, the airplane initially appeared impossible to repair in the field because its retractable antenna was too long to extend on the ground. That is, it had to be in the air to allow extension. The design flaw was easily solved, however, by digging a deep hole in the maintenance field.[46]

After the loss of one of the three JU-21As (Vanguard 216) to enemy fire, the men of the 138th Aviation Company committed their fallen comrades to memory and redistributed the workload,

The LEFT JAB direction-finding console.

A JU-21A undergoes a service check. Crew Chief Al Ellison is in prominent view. CPT Michael Marker sits in the cockpit while CPT Byron West inspects the wheel well.

now with only two LEFT JAB aircraft available. Yet, the loss of Vanguard 216 did not deter ARDF operations along the DMZ as the North Vietnamese might have expected. Instead, LEFT JAB met its requirement to operate at maximum output, most notably during the crucial phase of the 1972 Spring Offensive.[47]

As U.S. forces drew down in late 1972, the 138th Aviation Company relocated from Phu Bai to Da Nang, while continuing to meet all of its operational requirements. On 16 February 1973, LEFT JAB performed its last mission in the vicinity of Pleiku, South Vietnam. After the inactivation of the 138th Aviation Company, the two LEFT JAB systems were transferred to the aviation detachment of USASA Field Station Udorn in Thailand. They operated successfully in that unit until May 1975,

A JU-21A in its final years of service, reunited with the 138th Aviation Company in Orlando, Florida.

when the political situation precluded any further ARDF efforts in Southeast Asia. Remaining a valuable system, the JU-21As were transferred to the 156th Army Security Agency Company at Fort Bliss, Texas. In 1979, the systems were reunited with the 138th Army Security Agency Company, reactivated as a reserve unit in Orlando, Florida. Finally, in 1984, the company decommissioned LEFT JAB and transferred the two U-21s to the California National Guard for utility service.[48]

Using a JUH-1D helicopter, a LEFT BANK system operated in direct support of a tactical unit. Its distinctive "elephant brander" antenna can be seen mounted underneath the nose of the helicopter and extending forward.

The LEFT BANK patch of the 371st RR Company.

LEFT BANK

Fixed-wing platforms were not the only ARDF assets in Vietnam. ASA also designed systems for rotary-wing aircraft to round out the Army's airborne capability in-country. In 1967, five UH-1D Huey helicopters were equipped with AN/ANQ-27 intercept and direction-finding systems. ASA named this unique configuration LEFT BANK. Redesignated as the JUH-1D, the modified helicopter was recognizable by a nose-mounted, front-extending antenna, nicknamed an elephant brander. Three JUH-1Ds served under the 371st Radio Research (RR) Company to support the 1st Cavalry Division (Air Mobile) in the III Corps Tactical Zone. The crews referred to the title of a recent "spaghetti western" to name each platform: *The Good, The Bad, and The Ugly*. The two remaining JUH-1D helicopters served under the 374th Radio Research (RR) Company to support the 4th Infantry Division in the II Corps Tactical Zone. In 1969, the three JUH-1Ds of the 371st RR Company were replaced by UH-1Hs, which had greater payload capacity and engine power. The resulting LEFT BANK platforms went by designation JUH-1H.

In addition to its rotary-wing design, LEFT BANK was atypical among ASA airborne systems in other ways. First, it was a collaborative effort: ASA packaged each system and provided three operators while the helicopter, pilot, and co-pilot came directly from the supported unit. Second, the parent division had direct and exclusive operational control and tasking authority over the LEFT BANK system. By making it tactically responsive at the division level and below, ARDF could function effectively in a combined effort with the firepower and mobility of helicopter gunships.[49] In this way, onboard crews had the leeway to create and implement their own version of working directly with tactical fighting assets toward a common goal.

From the start, LEFT BANK was an unlikely system. Initial studies had demonstrated that rotary-wing platforms were less than adequate for ARDF. In 1963, however, the Stanford Research Institute (SRI) determined that ARDF was possible in a UH-1D, if a more complex system (one that allowed for dipole balance under dynamic conditions) could be built. The SRI study proved beneficial when ASA and EWL began their own developmental programs. Initially, the research teams developed a system with onboard navigation, ARDF, HF collection, and radio fingerprinting—audio identification—but after two years of operational testing, mission specialists realized that complexity was inherently problematic on helicopters.

SGT Thomas Hurth of the 371st RR Company demonstrates an ARDF console on LEFT BANK.

Autorotation saved a LEFT BANK crew but not without serious damage to the helicopter and equipment.

In final form, simplicity prevailed: LEFT BANK was reengineered into a single-function ARDF system to optimize direction-finding capabilities against enemy HF. As an added benefit, the characteristics of the rotary-wing system allowed for the installation of a "spaced loop" antenna, which had previously been used by ground direction-finding teams. Radio receivers using this antenna were most effective between four and eight megahertz, a range in which most targets of tactical importance operated.[50]

Operations were not without difficulty. Fundamentally, a working concept did not exist to integrate the capabilities of LEFT BANK with the firepower and mobility of air cavalry. From a technical perspective, without the more sophisticated navigational equipment in other ARDF platforms, LEFT BANK crews had to navigate using visual markers, distinguishable mostly at low altitudes. Because the system was already underpowered, personnel and equipment weights precluded the use of armor. The aviator, therefore, had no choice but to maintain higher altitude—between 1,000 and 2,000 feet— to defend against hostile ground fire.

The nature of helicopters also made LEFT BANK prone to equipment failure. Rust in brush recorders, oil seepage, and fiberglass cracks in the spaced loop antennae were common. Moreover, rotary-wing vibrations tested the stress levels on the system equipment and the platform. Maintenance assessments of the LEFT BANK-modified helicopters set their limit before retrograde at 2,000 hours, compared to 3,200 hours for regular UH-1s. The maintenance problem was compounded because the Army considered LEFT BANK equipment and logistics a special requirement. Furthermore, when maintenance was neglected, even routine preventative checks, the results could be catastrophic. This condition became all too evident one day when a JUH-1D under the 1st Cavalry Division (Air Mobile) experienced engine failure at 2,000 feet above the ground. Fortunately, the pilot was able to enter an emergency autorotation and skillfully brought his helicopter down. Although the skid hit a tree stump and the airframe landed on its side, no lives were lost, and its ARDF equipment was salvaged.[51]

Despite these obstacles, LEFT BANK proved an overwhelming success on the battlefield and provided the coverage to validate the concept of the hunter-killer team. According to a pilot of LEFT BANK and a platoon leader in the 1st Cavalry Division (Air Mobile) then Captain Carlos Collat, "division based strike teams of OH-6 scouts and AH-1 Cobras could now take advantage of the quickly passed ARDF emitter targets provided by LEFT BANK against these very threats that were operating essentially beneath the helicopters in the dense brush or tree lines previously overlooked."[52] In 1969, the two JUH-1D platforms of the 4th Infantry Division flew 315 missions (1,215 hours), which led to 438 fixes of slightly more than 400 meters in radius. In one month alone, the resulting information led to direct engagements that resulted in more than 300 enemy kills. To reduce the response times and establish a better operational concept, the brigade S2 extended the communication system to pink teams for expedited targeting, precluding the need for less accurate air and artillery bombardments. In the meantime, LEFT BANK would continue to narrow the fix, often detecting its exact location and vectoring forces into sight of the enemy. When the team discovered heavy concentrations of troops, an aero-rifle platoon was alerted for possible ground follow-up.[53]

Shortly after the start of LEFT BANK operations, Major General Elvy B. Roberts, the commanding general, 1st Cavalry Division (Air Mobile), became disenchanted with the system. He even considered withdrawing it on more than one occasion. By the end of his tour, however, he had become its most ardent supporter: "I cannot overstate the highly valuable intelligence, reported on a near real-time basis, that the Cav has accrued as a result of this splendid system."[54] Following an initial adjustment phase, LEFT BANK identified 234 targets and discovered fifty enemy staging areas within three months. More spectacular yet, as its single most significant accomplishment, air cavalry LEFT BANK operators of the 371st RR Company located "the city," the enemy's well-hidden logistics complex, supporting the Cambodian incursion of 1970. Upon securing the area, U.S. forces discovered 182 storage bunkers heavily loaded with caches of weapons and supplies.[55]

LEFT BANK's limited resources of only five helicopters in theater at any one time were always used to their fullest extent. In November 1970, when the 4th Infantry Division was preparing to return to Fort

In 1969, CPT Carlos Collat was assigned as the LEFT BANK platoon leader in the 371st RR Company, 1st Cavalry Division, call sign Jaguar Yellow. As a ground advisor to the ARVN in a previous tour, he observed the lack of timely and relevant intelligence to tactical forces. In his next tour, he saw the potential of LEFT BANK as a means to fix this problem. The system could locate enemy threats and quickly pass the data to division-level air and ground combat elements.

The LEFT BANK patch of the 265th RR Company.

Carson, Colorado, the LEFT BANK systems of the 374th RR Company were transferred to the 265th Radio Research Company of the 101st Airborne Division. As American involvement in Vietnam was drawing down, LEFT BANK assets were consolidated in the 405th Radio Research Detachment in January 1972. LEFT BANK continued to serve in Vietnam until 30 June 1972, when MACV finally withdrew the system.[56]

Considering the frequent dangerous missions and countless close calls, the pilots and crews had to "keep their heads" under extreme conditions. According to Collat, the enemy easily recognized LEFT BANK helicopters and, realizing their effectiveness, wanted to bring them down at any cost. For that reason, these unarmed and unarmored helicopters were extremely vulnerable to ground fire when their flight patterns became predictable and when the mission required low-flying profiles to narrow a target fix. Twice, LEFT BANK helicopters were shot down. In both cases, all onboard were lost. Their names were Chief Warrant Officer 2 Jack D. Knepp, Warrant Officer 1 Dennis D. Bogle, Private First Class Henry N. Heide II, Specialist 4 James R. Smith, Warrant Officer 1 Paul V. Black, Warrant Officer 1 Robert D. Uhl, Specialist 5 Gary C. David, and Specialist 4 Frank A. Sablan.[57]

The OV-1 Mohawk

While ASA demonstrated the advantages of ARDF in Vietnam, other aerial-intelligence disciplines were also moving forward. The more traditional forms of aerial reconnaissance, those akin to visual observation, retained their value, especially when they were augmented with new technologies. In 1950, the L-19 Bird Dog, a Cessna model, had replaced the O-59/L-4 as the Army's main short takeoff and landing aircraft for artillery spotting and tactical reconnaissance. Although the helicopter had usurped many of its missions through the late 1950s, the Bird Dog remained irreplaceable in the role of forward artillery observer.

In 1962, the Army upgraded the L-19-series aircraft to match new combat standards and changed its designation to O-1 to conform to a Department-of-Defense directive, which reflected its service in both the Army and Air Force. The first thirty-three O-1s to arrive in Vietnam went to the 73d Aviation Company (Light Air Surveillance) at Tan Son Nhut Air Base in May 1963. As the conflict escalated, the Army contracted with Cessna to produce 310 more O-1 variants. Altogether, they flew more than 30,000 combat hours, primarily for artillery spotting and forward air control.

Army and Air Force O-1s, side by side.

By the late 1960s, however, the Department of Defense reassigned most O-1s to the Air Force as part of a move to consolidate all forward air control duties within one service. Only a small number of these aircraft remained under the Army. Despite the loss of so many assets, the transfer had little effect on the Army's capabilities. As the war had progressed, helicopters had moved into their own as more versatile vehicles for reconnaissance in support of ground combat, but just as important, by the late 1960s, the Army had acquired and deployed a large number of OV-1 Mohawks for service in Vietnam.[58]

Impressed with the prototypes, the Army finally had what it had always wanted in a reconnaissance aircraft and authorized the purchase of 344 airplanes.[59] Two 960-horsepower Lycoming T-53 L-3 turboprop engines produced enough thrust to "attain a speed of 460 miles per hour at 20,000 feet," and a wingspan longer than the fuselage provided sufficient lift for 18,000 pounds of aircraft.[60] It could maintain an altitude of 25,000 feet but typically cruised at 16,000 feet at a considerably slower 240 miles per hour to avoid using stored oxygen.[61] Considered a small, mid-wing aircraft,

An unofficial Patch of the 23d Special Warfare Aviation Detachment.

Hot off the production line, one of the first OV-1As is moved to a holding area in Hampton, Virginia (1962).

the OV-1 was in a class by itself, able to do short takeoffs and landings and complete a 180-degree roll in one second. The pilots appreciated the Mohawk's tail section, a triple stabilizer layout. These three vertical fins replaced the original prototype's one to compensate for the incredible torque of the turboprop engines and to minimize shaking, thus enhancing the performance of sensitive equipment. This design change allowed the OV-1 to travel as slowly as the O-1 Bird Dog for extended observation at low altitudes.[62] Upon seeing the tail section, soldiers in Europe referred the Mohawk as the "triple-tailed devil."

Once called the most beautiful ugly aircraft, and compared to the appearance of a dragonfly, the Mohawk was a classic example of function dictating form. The Grumman Corporation designed the airframe's bulging bulbous cockpit with an enlarged glass canopy for the crew to have maximum visibility in contrast to the conventional streamlined design. The observer could look down from the side to see the ground almost directly below. Intended for operation on the frontline, the aerial platform was protected by armor or flak curtains, and its reduced radar cross section functioned as an early version of stealth.[63] The standard model had compartments and wing racks to carry 3,000 pounds of equipment. Its tanks could hold enough fuel for long missions of more than six hours or 900 miles.[64] Additionally, it was notable for other distinctive features: compact dimensions, Martin Baker ejection seats, a tricycle landing gear, and a bug-eyed nose cockpit for the pilot and observer to sit side by side.

The first variant of the Mohawk was designated as the OV-1A, of which sixty-four were manufactured. First based in West Germany, most were diverted to Vietnam immediately after production. Designed for visual observation and tactical PHOTINT, this type was equipped with the KS-61 Photographic System, consisting of two large-format cameras (that rotated from vertical to fifteen degrees of the horizon) on each wing and a 180-degree panoramic camera in the nose.[65] In December 1962, six of these aircraft, under the 23d Special Warfare Aviation Detachment, were the first of many Mohawks to enter service in Vietnam.

The versatility of the OV-1A and its performance record tempted many commanders to augment it with offensive capabilities. Indeed, within two years, the 11th Air Assault Division at Fort Benning, Georgia, received six modified Mohawks, redesignated as the JOV-1A, to become the first fixed-wing gunships under Army control since the Second World War. More would follow. The J stood for joint, used as a means to bypass possible objections from the Air Force, which emphatically

A JOV-1A Mohawk with its full complement of armaments.

and vigilantly guarded its monopoly on fixed-wing offensive aircraft. In 1965, the 11th Air Assault Division was reflagged as the 1st Cavalry Division (Air Mobile) and ordered to Vietnam. Less than a year later, twenty-seven JOV-1A gunships were flying close air support for MACV.[66]

The JOV-1A's reconnaissance attributes and weaponry proved a potent combination against enemy forces. It carried a combination of .50-caliber machine guns, 500-pound bombs, MK 24 flares, and 5-inch Zuni Rockets. The Viet Cong referred to this model as "the Whispering Death" because of its quiet approach and delivery of ordnance. In combat, a Mohawk could enter enemy territory at a low altitude, using hills and ridges to mask itself from radar, then pop up on its target at a higher altitude to make observations or launch an assault, thence dive back into the protection of the terrain. Its engines (also used on helicopters) allowed the aircraft to move slowly and quietly with a stall speed of sixty-three miles per hour. Success not only drew the attention of the enemy but also raised vociferous objections from the Air Force Staff in Washington, DC. According to the service's claims, the Army had violated the 1948 Key West Agreement, which assigned armed fixed-wing close air support exclusively to the Air Force.[67] The resulting interservice discord eventually put an end to the armed Mohawk.[68]

Fortunately for its advocates, the Mohawk's versatility seemed unlimited. The Army Concept Team in Vietnam (ACTIV) determined that the aircraft was more than satisfactory to observe guerrillas in counterinsurgency operations, noting its speed, range, maneuverability, survivability, and stealthy nature. By 1965, Grumman had delivered 90 OV-1Bs with wingspans extended from 42 to 48 feet to accommodate the AN/APS-94 Side-Looking Airborne Radar (SLAR) pod—an imaging radar system, mounted underneath and parallel to the fuselage. The pod was eighteen feet long, shaped like a canoe, and made of fiberglass. Reaching the end of their development cycles at close to the same time, SLAR and the Mohawk became a perfect match.

SLAR technology had progressed steadily in military service since its introduction in 1957. Older systems, such as the AN/APS-85 and AN/APQ-86, had been installed on military aircraft, including the RL-26D Aero Commander—later called the RU-9D—for experimentation and the U-8D Seminole—redesignated as either the RU-8D or RL-23D—for limited operational service in West Germany and South Korea. SLAR was based on the concept of transmitting pulses of radar at a relatively low angle towards the earth's surface. The system's antenna emitted radar signals perpendicular to the fuselage on

From top to bottom, an OV-1A, OV-1B, and OV-1C fly information.

Members of the Aerial Surveillance and Target Acquisition (ASTA) Platoon, 1st Cavalry Division (Air Mobile), prepare an OV-1B with SLAR for an operation in An Khe, Vietnam.

both sides of the surveillance aircraft as it travelled parallel to the battlefront. Radar waves penetrated foliage cover, day and night, and in most weather conditions. The resulting electromagnetic feedback (bounced signals) detected movement and revealed targets on the ground. The radar was a two-channel system of both fixed and moving target indication (MTI). The fixed channel provided a photographic map of terrain while MTI detected the movement of objects, such as armor, support vehicles, and artillery pieces, on the battlefield.[69] SLAR film was processed in flight, and the technical operator, sitting in the cockpit, had access to images through an electronic monitor.[70]

Other surveillance technologies continued to catch the Mohawk developer's imagination. Not long after the introduction of the B model, OV-1Cs arrived in theater with the AN/UAS-4 "Red Haze" Infrared (IR) Detection system as well as the standard KS-61 Photographic System. The AN/UAS-4 was an IR line-scan camera looking down from the fuselage, which provided units with advanced IMINT.[71] The IR sensor could detect both radiated and reflected "infrared energy."[72] To expedite the transference of this time-sensitive intelligence, the Army provided ground sensor terminals with OV-1Bs and Cs.[73] Designed to serve division-level headquarters, these datalinked stations received transmissions from SLAR and IR sensors, converted the incoming data into imagery, and thereby produced near real-time information of detected targets while the aircraft were flying. Unfortunately for U.S. forces in Vietnam, these terminals were

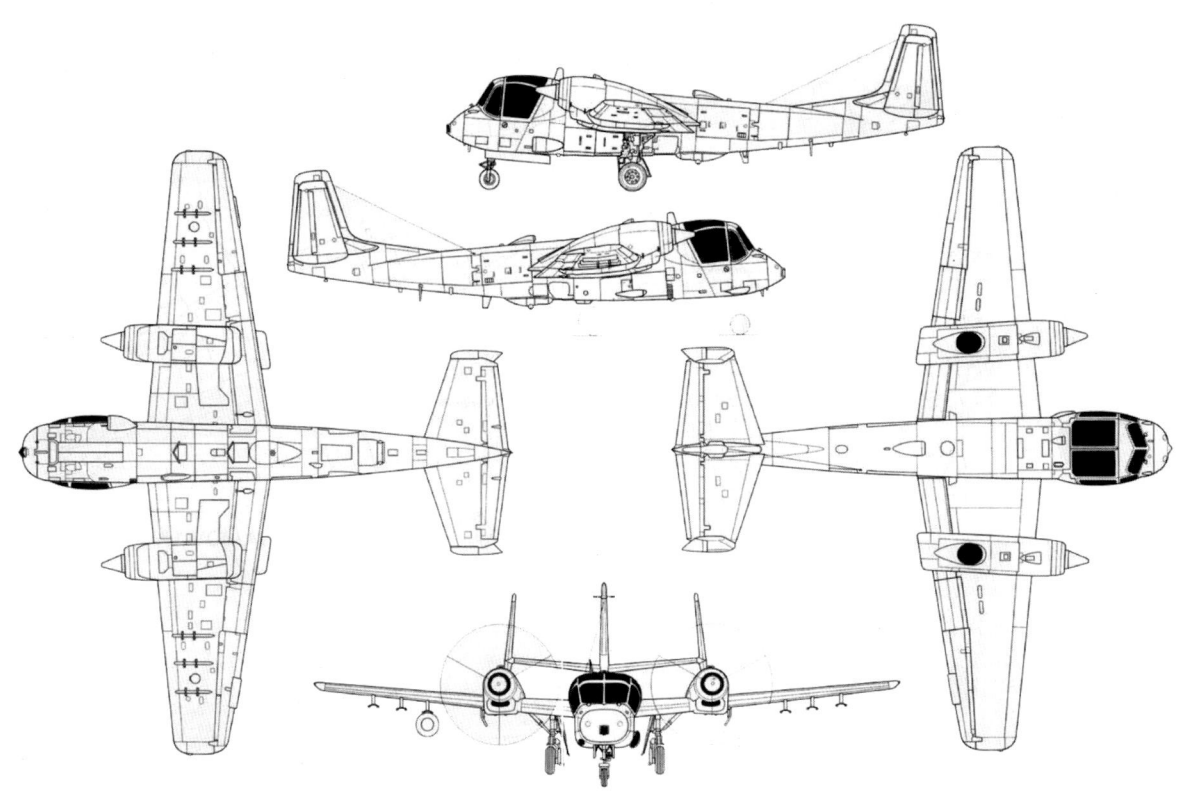

A dimensional representation of the OV-1D.

neither available in sufficient quantities nor operationally reliable, but as the technology matured, Army units worldwide would come to appreciate later versions.[74]

One-hundred and sixty-five "C" models were built of which thirty-two were converted to JOV-1C gunships.[75] By 1967, the Army had fifty-nine JOV-1A and C conversions. It was at this time that the Secretary of Defense Robert S. McNamara placed a moratorium on more armed Mohawks, eventually ending in their outright disarmament. As the weaponized role for this aircraft was coming to an end, the Army aimed to introduce an all-purpose version by combining the functions of the OV-1A, B, and C into one model, the OV-1D. After producing thirty-seven off the assembly line, from late 1968 onward, the Army converted all of its previous models into OV-1Ds. This new unarmed Mohawk became the standard.

As the conflict in Vietnam escalated, what started as Mohawk detachments were consolidated, integrated, and restructured into companies at the division level. In the new organizational system, Mohawks were flying in five companies: the 73d, 131st, 225th, 244th, and 245th Aviation Companies (Aerial Surveillance) under the call signs of Warriors, Spuds, Phantom Hawks, Delta Hawks, and Red Eyes, respectively. In these units, the Army better managed this intelligence asset for logistics and control. Their success also brought casualties. Sixty-six Mohawks were lost in Vietnam: thirty-six from operational accidents and thirty from enemy fire.[76]

Soldiers commonly remarked that the Mohawk was one of the ugliest airplanes ever built but admired its inner beauty on the battlefield. Encapsulating this point, an aircraft mechanic once said, "[i]t's not real pretty to look at but it's a beautiful aircraft."[77] With regard to its resilience, he went on to comment, "[i]t can take about anything the weather throws at it and still fly."[78] In combat the Mohawk was especially robust. During a particularly eventful mission, Major Joseph Kennedy's OV-1A was hit by a Vietnamese 37mm anti-aircraft gun. As flames gushed out of what was left of the fuselage, he managed to bring the aircraft back to base. After landing, the elevator cable was released, causing the tail assembly to fall apart on the runway. As Paul Reed, an executive director of the Mohawk Association, remembered, "uncounted VC and NVA had their morning rice mixed with artillery, fired on coordinates provided by IR equipped Mohawks. Trucks on the Ho Chi Minh Trail, vessels at sea and encampments under seemingly impenetrable jungle all were Mohawk targets."[79]

Army Aerial Intelligence at Vietnam's End

At 0800 hours on 28 January 1973, the ceasefire in Vietnam took effect. The drawdown was already underway. Not long after, on 16 February, a LEFT JAB crew flew its final mission in the vicinity of Pleiku for the 138th Aviation Company, and the Lonely Ringer Battalion, symbolically concluded the Army's first exploration in airborne SIGINT with its host of technologies. ARDF units were among the least known serving in Vietnam, yet by any measure, they were the most valuable of Army intelligence assets. If historians were to describe the American involvement in Vietnam as a military setback, aerial intelligence, surveillance, and reconnaissance would be the exception. It was more successful than anyone could have imagined and proved worthy of further experimentation and investment.[80]

Even before the conflict drew to a close, ASA and the Army Staff had plans to capitalize on the recent technological advancements in aerial intelligence for the benefit of U.S. forces worldwide. What worked as a tactical solution to the problems of irregular warfare in Vietnam might have potential against a wider range of military challenges. The designers would refer to the next generation of systems by a collective name, Special Electronic Mission Aircraft (SEMA).

*As the deadline approached and with limited space
in the project buildings, programmers found themselves working
on the equipment at midnight under streetlamps in the parking lot.
One trying moment came when a cricket managed to get into a card feeder,
which completely jammed the machinery.—*

*The 7th RR Field Station at Udorn Royal Thai Air Force Base, Thailand served as the center
for the Army ARDF effort in Southeast Asia after the drawdown in Vietnam.*

CHAPTER THREE

GUARDRAIL and a New Look for Intelligence

From Vietnam to the Birth of GUARDRAIL

The 1973 ceasefire in Vietnam was an end with mixed results for U.S. policy. The North Vietnamese presence remained intact while American support to South Vietnamese forces was reduced substantially. For the Army, the agreement assured an orderly withdrawal from the country. Only two years later, Saigon fell to advancing Marxist forces. In the meantime, Army resourcing reverted to the more enduring objective—the defense of Western Europe. Compensating for neglect during the Vietnam conflict, U.S. military emphasis returned to strengthening and modernizing NATO forces. This policy shift was complicated by the end of the draft in 1972 and the return of a volunteer service the next year.

As part of the Army's drawdown in Vietnam, ASA proceeded with the incremental relocation of its forces, including its remaining aerial-intelligence assets. Most airborne-SIGINT systems still in service after the 138th Aviation Company's inactivation were transported out of Vietnam but remained in theater. From 1973 to 1975, both LEFT JAB and LAFFING EAGLE systems operated in an aviation detachment as part of the 7th Radio Research Field Station at Udorn Royal Thai Air Force Base, Thailand (later transferred to the closer U-Tapao Royal Thai Air Force Base). Thence, crews tracked guerrilla movements from Vietnam into Cambodia and Laos. This effort matched the success of the Vietnam missions. The deteriorating political situation in Cambodia, however, eventually led to its cancellation. In May 1975, ASA disbanded the aviation detachment; its personnel and equipment returned to the United States. The aircraft, after maintenance in California, were transferred to the 156th ASA Company at Fort Bliss, Texas.[1]

Even while the Vietnam conflict was still raging, the Army continued to improve aerial-intelligence systems in support of countering the long-standing threat of Soviet aggression in Western Europe. Unlike the conditions in Vietnam, the Army leadership in the European theater at first saw no great need for airborne COMINT. In this static environment, ASA achieved satisfactory results by relying

Aircrews of the aviation detachment at the 7th RR Field Station pose in front of a JU-21A LEFT JAB aircraft.

on a network of field stations. ELINT, on the other hand, remained an intelligence challenge and invited possibilities for aerial collection. Beginning in 1961, as noted in the first chapter, ASA used airborne SIGINT for short-lived systems with such names as BATTLEAXE, HOT PIPE, SILVER LANCE, SURE THING and GOFER DELTA. In 1973, the Army transferred to ASA an advanced program called QUICK LOOK, involving electronic sensors mounted on two OV-1C Mohawks to intercept and locate radars. Later versions of this SEMA system, QUICK LOOK IA and QUICK LOOK II, proved invaluable as part of a larger ELINT package from which NATO forces were able to map the placement of Soviet radar units.[2]

One of two OV-1Cs equipped with the QUICK LOOK I package.

In 1970, while the U.S. Army Troop Support and Aviation Readiness Command was testing QUICK LOOK, it occurred to the ASA leadership in Europe that something conceptually similar could be applied to solve the troublesome problem of intercepting the line-of-sight, tactical communications of Warsaw Pact forces and delivering the collected, highly perishable information to the appropriate opposing NATO units.[3] The Warsaw Pact tactical ground and air forces frequently communicated with low-powered line-of-sight radios. The field stations that ASA operated in Europe and Turkey were unable to intercept these low-powered signals beyond the radio horizon, and even if they could, the tactical nature of these signals precluded the possibility of a field station, designed for strategic intercept, relaying information in a timely manner.

To fill this COMINT gap, the ASA staff would have to meet a series of objectives. First and most important would be determining the best method of interception, which, in this case, could only come from aerial exploitation. Second, a program would require the service of an experienced SEMA manufacturer. Third, the mission would require the simultaneous use of multiple aircraft. Fourth, information would have to transfer almost instantly from air to ground. Fifth, tactical units would need connectivity to make use of time-sensitive intelligence; this would entail some means of mobile relay.[4]

An RU-21G GUARDRAIL I in flight provides a clear view of its VHF T/R Antenna in front of the tail section.

On behalf of ASA and United States European Command (USEUCOM), the acting Chairman of the Joint Chiefs of Staff, General Westmoreland, solicited help from the Director, National Security Agency (NSA), on 26 January 1971, to develop a SEMA system based on those objectives. In response, Charles Gandy, the chief of a developmental section of NSA called R-24, proposed a plan and obtained approval to produce an experimental model. NSA categorized the subsequent program as a quick reaction capability (QRC)—a process by which recently matured technologies are expeditiously developed into systems for service in the field. The agency then awarded a four-million-dollar contract to Electronic Systems Laboratories (ESL), an agile and reputable technology firm, to furnish a system capable of receiving ultra-high frequency (UHF) and VHF signals. The program's name would be GUARDRAIL. Gandy took over as its leader, while Colonel Norman Campbell assumed the role of test director. The Army insisted on a finished product from ESL within five-and-a-half months.

As the deadline approached and with limited space in the project buildings, programmers found themselves working on the equipment at midnight under streetlamps in the parking lot. One trying moment came when a cricket managed to get into a card feeder, which completely jammed the

102

machinery. Despite such nuisances, ESL managed to outfit one ground station, two jeep-mounted remote relays, and three specially modified variants of the U-21 aircraft—redesignated as the RU-21G.[5] The test result was a breakthrough on the same proportions as the invention of ARDF. For the first time, the aircraft carried no operators. All collected information was relayed to the ground station, called an Integrated Processing Facility (IPF), for analysis and then disseminated through a secure datalink. In a sense, the aircraft became an antenna for the ground station receiver.

After assembly, ASA transported the aircraft and system to El Paso, Texas, to develop sustainment and testing procedures before deployment. The U.S. Army Aviation Electronic Warfare (EW) Company was charged with this task. Before the arrival of GUARDRAIL, this specialized unit had been preparing CEFIRM LEADER, the next in a line of systems belatedly destined for Vietnam. For the pilots, technicians, and operators, many of whom had just returned from ARDF missions in Southeast Asia, GUARDRAIL was unlike anything they had seen before. It was the cutting edge of the Army's next generation of airborne SIGINT, demonstrating an intercept range and a frequency reception far superior to any system previously fielded. More important, they realized that SEMA was more than a

The USA Aviation Electronic Warfare Company temporarily became the caretaker of GUARDRAIL for preparation and testing.

The first RU-21E LEFT FOOT system rolled out of production in 1972, too late for its intended use in Vietnam.

countermove to irregular warfare and that it had utility beyond Vietnam. These veterans also appreciated the great benefit of keeping the operators on the ground and wondered if this new developmental project could be destined to serve on the frontline of the Cold War. At the time, however, they were also puzzled to observe that GUARDRAIL was a system without ARDF.[6]

In August 1971, GUARDRAIL left the U.S. to join the yearly REFORGER exercise in Europe. Colonel Campbell headed the operation, and an ASA flight detachment of aviators (mostly veterans of the 224th Aviation Battalion) flew the missions. The RU-21Gs were based at Hanau Army Airfield and Ramstein Air Base, typically flying west of the Rhine River. The IPF operated out of an old Nike missile site at Grundstadt, West Germany. Inside its two trailers, each forty feet long, operators remotely tuned the UHF/VHF intercept receivers in each aircraft and listened over a secure datalink. Useful information was forwarded to tactical units through mobile relay systems.

The experiment could only have been described as a success so much so that ASA kept the experimental equipment in theater for regular operations until modifications were required. Indeed, GUARDRAIL continued its deployment for three months. For the first time, the Army had a SIGINT battlefield surveillance system, as a corps-level asset, which could support theater-level requirements. The results encouraged developers to make the next logical step by adding an ARDF system.[7]

GUARDRAIL II: The Next Step

Repeating their original cooperative arrangement, ASA, NSA, ESL and the Beech Aircraft Company began the development of GUARDRAIL II for the 1972 REFORGER exercise. Once again, ESL delivered in less than six months. The critical problem in developing this SEMA product was designing a remotely operated ARDF system. Initial testing began with antennae attached to an engineer's personal automobile but ended with a final ARDF product, tested in a Beech aircraft.

Part of the solution came from repurposing six of sixteen RU-21E LEFT FOOT aircraft, designed and built to serve in Vietnam. LEFT FOOT was an improved version of LAFFING EAGLE with the same computer system used in LEFT JAB. The drawdown in Vietnam precluded their deployment and prompted the reassignment of the LEFT FOOT systems to the 156th ASA Company (Aviation) (Fixed Wing) at Fort Bliss. The two-position HF/VHF radio direction-finding capability already installed on the RU-21Es proved well-adapted for GUARDRAIL.[8] As the next generation of GUARDRAIL SEMA, their new aircraft designation was RU-21H.

Constructing a GUARDRAIL airframe was no simple task. After choosing the aircraft for conversion, the process began by taking them to a Beech Aircraft facility in Wichita, Kansas, for modification. At that time, ASA chose a team of aviators to accompany these airplanes through the entire process of conversion and delivery to West Germany. For the pilots, Wichita was a memorable location as they witnessed the reconfiguration of their aircraft to become GUARDRAIL platforms by day and fortified their comradeship by night over beverages at the local bar called the Red Lion. Having served the pilots of the first GUARDRAIL project, the Red Lion reached the status of a tradition early on, and its logo, displayed on the pilots' hats, had already become an emblem to symbolize the broader mission. The Institute of Heraldry was not to know that the ferocity and cunning of the lion had nothing to do with the inspiration for the unit insignia of the GUARDRAIL company formed a year later in West Germany. After receipt of the aircraft, the pilots' first mission was a flight to Moffett Naval Air Station in California for installation of the electronic equipment and calibration.

Calibration challenged the aviators' skills while flying in the congested airspace of the San Francisco Bay area. Flight tracks lasted more than three hours and, at times, overlapped various commercial flight routes. Keeping contact with air control was a serious matter. Intersecting with one particular track, a Pacific Southwest Airlines (PSA) flight was advised that a GUARDRAIL aircraft was flying at

The red lion would come to symbolize GUARDRAIL II in its formative years.

The final version of the RU-21H GUARDRAIL II system.

The oxygen mask was a fixture of GUARDRAIL aviation in the 1970s.

20,000 feet, approaching from the twelve o'clock position. The airline pilot's response was "what's a GUARDRAIL?" The GUARDRAIL pilot on the same frequency then responded by asking "what's a PSA?" Many years later, those Army pilots could not help but acknowledge the irony in discovering that PSA went out of business at a time when GUARDRAIL was in a phase of rapid growth.[9]

Once calibration was complete, the next objective brought them back to Wichita for the installation of extra fuel tanks to make their long journey to Europe. For some of these flyers, this mission was their second time transporting GUARDRAIL to West Germany. The U-21 had no autopilot for the long hours of uneventful flying, which occurred on ferrying journeys as well as on operational missions. The first GUARDRAIL contingent required seven legs of flying to reach another continent, and no aviator could understate the physical stresses in thin air. The military version of the King Air had no internal pressurization, which made high-altitude flight reminiscent of missions in World War II. The cockpits were freezing, and pressure was low. For GUARDRAIL to be effective, the RU-21 had to reach an altitude that required oxygen from a tank and special suits, including insulated footwear, universally known in the services as Mickey Mouse boots. Pilots were directly exposed to these conditions for long durations, experiencing symptoms of the bends: an achy body was the least of their worries as nitrogen bubbles would settle in their knees.[10]

CPT Carlos Collat and CPT Christopher Curkendall prepare in the GUARDRAIL II flight operations center at Hanau, West Germany.

For the mission commander, Major Donald Stewart, the trip was the second time he had led GUARDRAIL from one side of the Atlantic to the other. Crews were paired up based on experience. Supervising three more aircraft than on his first GUARDRAIL ferrying mission a year earlier, Stewart determined that the group should fly in a formation, an option that would allow one airplane to represent all six to the air traffic controller instead of having six individual aircraft in direct communication.

The destination of their first leg was Dulles Airport, Virginia, where the crews acquired over-water gear, such as parachutes and life rafts. On the next leg, heading for Bangor, Maine, unexpected weather broke up the formation, leading to a scramble to obtain individual clearances for landing. Avoiding a predicament, the crews, who had flown in Vietnam, responded by maneuvering in a concerted effort to different altitudes and in different directions until individual landings were complete. Nevertheless, all participants agreed that this type of mission was not suited for formations. It was a lesson learned without loss because careful flying prevented any serious consequences.

After an uneventful flight to Goose Bay, Labrador, the landing of the next leg at Sondrestrom, Greenland, was unforgiving as the pilots had to fly up a fjord to reach the runway. There was no way to turn back if environmental or mechanical conditions proved untenable. Fortunately, the weather worked to their advantage. The aviators were not so lucky upon approach to Keflavik, Iceland, when the airplanes hit high-velocity winds, reaching sixty knots. Having no margin for error and flying in the darkness of night, aviators had to feel their way through the wind, and a momentary break in judgment could have led to disaster. As the last aircraft approached the runway, wind gusts changed direction. The aircrew had to abort landing at the last possible moment and use additional power against the headwinds on the alternate runway.

Then came the heavy fog approaching Mildenhall, England, but it was nothing compared to the visibility issues at their final destination in West Germany at Hanau Army Airfield, Fliegerhorst Kaserne. The runway was short. In fact, some aviation units refused to use it, which explained its relatively easy availability for GUARDRAIL. During World War II, the Luftwaffe stationed its advanced jets there to take advantage of the fog for concealment. For some of the newer aviators on that mission, it was their first opportunity to witness a landing with zero ceiling and zero visibility. Indeed, an observer on the ground could have erroneously concluded that these airplanes brought the latest navigational landing equipment instead of GUARDRAIL. The end of their flight marked the establishment of a flying route that would sustain GUARDRAIL and other airborne MI systems in Europe for decades.[11]

The six RU-21Hs and the IPF arrived ready for the 1972 REFORGER exercise. Above 20,000 feet, the aircraft repeated a route, called a track, between Kiel in the north and Nuremberg in the south. Although the flying could be monotonous, the pilots appreciated the exposure to a new intelligence system. With the added direction-finding equipment, including multiple antennae, the aircraft, resembling flying porcupines, flew in pairs to engage collection and ARDF. On the ground, they traded their flight helmets for caps with the red lion insignia.[12]

The final product was a great technological leap forward. Airborne sensors intercepted selected frequencies on the radio spectrum from 250 to 350 miles away. From receivers on the ground, linguists scanned these intercepts to determine if they met reporting criteria. If so, they relayed the processed information—translated into English—back to the GUARDRAIL aircraft for instantaneous broadcast to tactical consumers. The transmission process, protected by an encryption system, would transpire in less than five minutes.[13]

On those long flights, the aviators had opportunities to add their own improvements, sometimes testing their skill and creativity. On a particular high-altitude mission, as a case in point, Captain Christopher Curkendall and Captain Carlos Collat experimented with their velocity against headwinds by advancing the props to full-forward pitch and "cracking" the flaps. The resulting reduced airspeed, slightly above a stall, into headwinds of over one-hundred knots, slowed the aircraft down to "floating"

The RU-21H instrument panel: "115 knots at flight level 230."

in a reversed direction along the same exact flight track using the same navigation points. Upon reaching their turning point, they increased velocity slightly beyond the opposing headwinds to move forward, again while remaining on the same route. This maneuver reduced the repetitive number of disruptive turns necessary to stay on a track. Furthermore, as long as the antennae remained level, this type of unconventional flying prolonged connectivity with the IPF and time on station, reduced fuel consumption, and increased mission effectiveness. The only drawback was that the aircraft's ram air heaters did not always engage at low airspeeds, compelling the need to keep more insulated flight clothing on hand.

After six months of testing, USEUCOM submitted an evaluation report to the Joint Chiefs of Staff dated 14 June 1974, recommending retention of the system in Europe. Having proven itself to field commanders, following a brief return to the U.S. for updating and recalibration, GUARDRAIL II received a logistical support package and was renamed GUARDRAIL IIA for permanent assignment in the European theater. To operate and maintain this new system, the Army had already organized the 330th Army Security Agency (ASA) Company (Aviation) (GUARDRAIL) under the 502d Army

ESL built six Mobile Relay Facilities (MRFs) in the early 1970s. Positioned high on the hills along the German border, each MRF had direction-finding and collection capabilities as a complementary collection system to that of GUARDRAIL II. The MRF had a datalink to the GUARDRAIL II IPF to exchange information and communicate with the aircraft. The Army eliminated the MRFs in the late 1970s due to budgetary and programmatic cuts in accordance with the Communications Electronic Warfare Intelligence (CEWI) concept.

Security Agency (ASA) Group on 5 November 1973.

Once operational, GUARDRAIL IIA began receiving assignments from U.S. Army Europe (USAREUR), the tactical SIGINT tasking authority. Wisely, USAREUR utilized all of the system's assets for coverage of Warsaw Pact military forces and featured it prominently in REFORGER exercises 74, 75, and 76. Colonel Campbell could rest assured that GUARDRAIL was no longer an experiment but rather an integrated system on an Army table of organization and equipment. In other words, as Carlos Collat observed, GUARDRAIL's "developmental auspices transferred from NSA to the Army."[14] Symbolically, the transfer would complete itself when the ASA eagle replaced the red lion on the 330th ASA Company's distinctive unit patch a few years later.

GUARDRAIL Goes to Korea

The irrefutable success of GUARDRAIL naturally spurred ASA planners to consider its application in other theaters, especially one where the possibility of attack always seemed imminent. Early in 1973, NSA proposed installing the latest GUARDRAIL equipment on six more of the 156th ASA Company's RU-21E LEFT FOOT aircraft and sending them to Korea as part of a project known as AIRBORNE ADVENTURER. Its antecedent—ADVENTURER—had been a system of ground-based remote relay sites setup in South Korea to intercept line-of-sight tactical and logistical communications from opposing forces. Colonel Campbell considered these sites a step in the evolution of line-of-sight intercept technology and a forerunner of GUARDRAIL.

Not long after the aerial project began, its original name was forgotten in favor of GUARDRAIL IV. (GUARDRAIL III never went beyond the testing phase because technological enhancements made its concept obsolete.) Like the procurement of GUARDRAIL II, more RU-21Es were converted into RU-21Hs. In addition, ESL created more advanced software and added a number of new hardware components: quick relays, automated direction finding, auxiliary ground equipment, improved datalinks, expanded VHF receivers, and teleprinters. Testing lasted from June to October 1974.[15]

Meanwhile, in South Korea, the 146th Aviation Company was reactivated on 1 July 1974. Redesignated as the 146th Army Security Agency (ASA) Company (Aviation) (GUARDRAIL IV), it was stationed at Pyong Taek and placed under the command and control of U.S. Army Security

MG James Ursano's panel recommended a fundamental restructuring of Army intelligence.

Agency Field Station Korea at Camp Humphreys, South Korea. On 6 November, the aviation unit's main body established residence at K-2 Air Base, in southwestern South Korea, near the town of Taegu, 150 miles southwest of the field station. The aircraft arrived at that location between February and March of 1975.

After testing, installation, and training, GUARDRAIL IV flew its first mission against enemy targets on 22 April. To the surprise of some, but not to its designers and operators, the aerial system exceeded expectations. Its receivers, operating at 20,000 feet, could penetrate far deeper than any of the ADVENTURER remote sites. Indeed, NSA operations representatives noted that GUARDRAIL IV was superior in quality when compared to other forms of tactical SIGINT in theater.[16]

Intelligence Takes on a New Look

While the early 1970s had witnessed major SEMA successes, military intelligence as a whole had fallen under scrutiny with the rest of the Army, partially brought about by a series of national misfortunes, all of which culminated in 1975. The fall of Saigon to North Vietnam, followed by Marxist regime changes in Laos and Cambodia, marked a failure of U.S. policy in Southeast Asia. The Watergate

MG William I. Rolya, the first commanding general of INSCOM (first row, fourth from the left), presides over the first INSCOM Commanders' Conference in 1978. ASA, later INSCOM, headquarters, Arlington Hall Station, in Arlington, Virginia.

scandal concluded with the end of a presidency and the loss of national confidence in its leadership. Soviet-backed insurrections came to power in Mozambique and Angola. Finally, the recent energy crisis and the politics of OPEC made 1975 a sobering year for Western nations. For the Army, now underfunded, unpopular, and without a draft, there was little promise for recruitment and acquisition.

These unfortunate circumstances bled into military intelligence. In 1974, Secretary of the Army Howard H. Calloway, in a memorandum to the Army Chief of Staff, General Frederick C. Weyand, raised doubts about the cost-effectiveness of the Army intelligence system. ASA began to have difficulties filling its ranks after the termination of the draft. The U.S. Army Intelligence Command—the Army's primary authority for counterintelligence—was in the process of being dismantled, partially as a result of a controversial past brought to light by accusations of spying on U.S. citizens. Furthermore, only one year earlier, Army intelligence resources had been reduced on a grand scale by the secretary of defense. Moreover, Weyand acknowledged that organizational reform was necessary across the entire Army. Consequently, he commissioned a panel of senior officers under the chairmanship of Major General Joseph J. Ursano to evaluate Army intelligence and submit recommendations for reorganization.

In August 1975, Ursano presented the panel's findings and recommendations to the Army Staff in a comprehensive report called the Intelligence Organization and Stationing Study (IOSS). According to its conclusions, intelligence production was fragmented, security assets were disproportionate,

ASA, later INSCOM, headquarters, Arlington Hall Station, in Arlington, Virginia.

and many functions of ASA had become redundant with the organization of the National Security Agency's Central Security Service (NSA/CSS). Even more serious, IOSS revealed a lack of resources in ASA to support all of the divisions in the Army. Additionally, Ursano's panel determined that tactical commanders were readily capable of assuming control of ASA field support units. Thus, in view of these discoveries, the IOSS recommendations included restructuring ASA, centralizing intelligence elements above corps, and decentralizing those below.

Secretary Calloway authorized a reform program based on Ursano's proposals to begin in 1976. ASA SIGINT units were combined with other MI units in the field or simply placed under their supported commanders. The Army then reorganized ASA to support MI units at echelons above corps (EAC) and proclaimed its new designation as the U.S. Army Intelligence and Security Command (INSCOM), effective on 1 January 1977. Its headquarters remained at Arlington Hall Station, Virginia. This meant the end of ASA's venerated, vertical command structure in favor of an interdisciplinary approach from tactical MI units up to the Department of the Army.

Later in 1977, the Army Staff began making transfers of major proportion. First, INSCOM assumed authority for counterintelligence in the continental United States. Second, the Army assigned production units, formerly under U.S. Army Forces Command (FORSCOM) and the Assistant Chief of

Officers and enlisted of the 156th ASA Company, Fort Bliss, Texas, in formation before an RU-21E LEFT FOOT.

Staff for Intelligence, to INSCOM. Many of these production units were consolidated under INSCOM's Intelligence Threat and Analysis Center (ITAC). Third, training, personnel, research and development, material acquisition, and administrative functions, formerly under the responsibility of ASA, went to other major Army commands or to the Army Staff. Finally, INSCOM assumed the command of three theater units: the 66th MI Group in West Germany from USAREUR (Seventh Army); the 470th MI Group in Panama from FORSCOM; and the 500th MI Group in Japan from the U.S. Army Intelligence Agency. As INSCOM historian John P. Finnegan remarked, "[t]he new command provided Army Intelligence with a framework within which the individual intelligence disciplines could cross-cue one

RU-21 CEFIRM LEADER aircraft stand ready for service as assets of the 1st ASA Company (Aviation).

another; the results of this collective effort would be greater than the sum of its parts."[17]

This new multi-disciplined approach to intelligence profoundly affected MI aviation. The most apparent outcome came from the dissolution of ASA. Its airborne-SIGINT units found themselves dispersed and reassigned to new organizations. In Europe, the 330th ASA Company (Aviation) (Forward), operating the GUARDRAIL IIA system, was reassigned to USAREUR and the Seventh Army. Under this new arrangement, GUARDRAIL came under the direct control of its service component commander in theater. In the United States, the 156th ASA Company (Aviation) (Fixed Wing) at Fort Bliss, Texas, and its parent organization, the 504th Army Security Agency Group, were placed under the command of FORSCOM. The 1st ASA Company (Aviation) (formerly a part of the 224th Aviation Battalion in Vietnam), which had only just been activated on 15 December 1975, assumed the responsibilities of the recently inactivated U.S. Army Aviation Electronic Warfare Company at Fort Bliss, and was also assigned to FORSCOM as part of the reorganized 504th MI Group.

Unrelated to this redistribution of units, but equally important, the 138th Army Security Agency

Reservists of the 138th ASA Company (Aviation)(Reserve) in Orlando, Florida, during the mid-1970s.

(ASA) Company (Aviation) (Reserve), was activated on 15 April 1974 at McCoy Air Force Base, Orlando, Florida, and assigned to the 81st U.S. Army Reserve Command.[18] This company, in reserve status, would have significance to INSCOM as the only aerial-intelligence unit in the Army dedicated to low intensity missions. Starting with RU-8D WINEBOTTLE aircraft and then picking up more advanced systems, the reservists performed an essential function at a lower cost to the Army in the succeeding decade.

Reservists of the 138th ASA Company (Aviation)(Reserve) conduct standard maintenance of an RU-8D WINEBOTTLE.

In South Korea, the 146th ASA Company (Aviation) (GUARDRAIL IV) was assigned to INSCOM on 1 January 1977. Its inheritance of this single aviation resource, followed by the acquisition in July of the 704th Military Intelligence Detachment (Aerial Surveillance), an airborne-IMINT unit also in South Korea, initiated the beginning of INSCOM's involvement in aerial intelligence. From this foothold, INSCOM would gradually expand over the next thirty years from having one company to holding the monopoly on all aerial intelligence in the Army. Thus, the command's humble beginnings in aviation were an unlikely prelude to an expansive future.

It felt like it was every mile of 8,000 miles away.

—D. ROBERTS

*The armistice, which was not followed by
any formal peace agreement, suggested that the cessation
of hostilities was only a pause to reload…—*

*It was like the 4th of July. So many sparks flew.
The sleeve completely disintegrated.
And the spray of molten connector pieces burned
some of the guy ropes supporting the antennas.
Antennas were falling like trees!*

—M. BUNTY

CHAPTER FOUR:
Walking the Line in Korea

At its start, INSCOM could not claim to be a substantial player in Special Electronic Mission Aircraft (SEMA) or aerial intelligence. Most of ASA's aerial assets had gone to either FORSCOM or USAREUR. The only exception was INSCOM's 146th ASA Company in the Korean theater. The unit's GUARDRAIL capability, however, was the equal to its counterpart in Europe, but the location was one of the most volatile, unpredictable, and precarious of the Cold War. For support personnel, considering their limitations at that time, INSCOM's one aviation company was no less a challenge than supporting a specialized brigade. In essence, the problem was geography. That is, INSCOM's first aviation unit was eight-thousand miles away from Arlington Hall Station at the end of a long military supply chain, running through the continental United States and the Pacific Ocean. As one INSCOM aviation officer commented, "[i]t felt like it was every mile of 8,000 miles away."[1]

A Large Threat on a Small Peninsula

Since the end of the Korean War in 1953, the atmosphere on the peninsula was perpetually restless. The armistice, which was not followed by any formal peace agreement, suggested that the cessation of hostilities was only a pause to reload and reposition the many weapons on both sides. Following the ceasefire, the United Nations and Communist Bloc agreed upon a Military Demarcation Line (MDL) roughly along the 38th parallel between the Soviet-backed Democratic People's Republic of Korea (DPRK) to the north and the U.S.-backed Republic of Korea (ROK) to the south. From the MDL both sides consented to move their troops back 2,000 meters, establishing a Demilitarized Zone (DMZ) four kilometers wide horizontally across the peninsula.

Formally still at war, owing to a stalemate and an irreconcilable hostility between North and South, large numbers of troops and equipment were stationed just outside the DMZ, ready to move. The armistice agreement defined in precise detail what military personnel and weapons were allowed

Since 1953, talks have been ongoing at the Joint Security Area, the only location where opposing forces maintain open contact on the Demilitarized Zone (DMZ). As the sight of the Armistice and subsequent negotiations, Panmunjom is commonly called "the truce village."

in the DMZ—not crossing the MDL—which, for the most part, would consist of small patrols to guard against surprise attack. To facilitate negotiations, both sides agreed to one connection point between North and South, designated as the Joint Security Area (JSA) near the western coast at Panmunjom. Opposing forces would maintain a number of buildings on their respective sides of the MDL within the JSA. Some structures were positioned to have shared space; indeed, for a time, the line even divided the conference rooms and tables right down the middle where parties from North Korea and the United Nations Command would infrequently meet face to face.[2]

Over the decades, the armistice has remained in effect over the DMZ. It was not so completely demilitarized, however, as the name suggests: infrequent skirmishes occurred between patrols. One such skirmish even occurred on the grounds of the JSA. Rarely accidental, these encounters were initiated by North Korean raids on U.S. and ROK patrols in or along the DMZ. A publicized attack of this type occurred in 1969, killing four U.S. soldiers. In 1974, South Koreans discovered a tunnel under the DMZ with electric lines, lamps, and a railway. Not even a year later, they discovered a second tunnel, deeper underground, only reinforcing suspicions of imminent surprise attack from the north. Following an incursion by North Korea in 1976, which left three North Koreans and six South Koreans dead, a U.S. attempt to remove tree branches from an obscured view in the JSA caused a skirmish, killing two American soldiers. Before this occurrence (often called the "tree trimming incident"), soldiers of both sides were permitted to traverse the MDL inside the JSA during negotiations. This privilege was revoked thereafter.

Volatility was not limited to the DMZ. In 1968, North Korean naval forces boarded and captured the USS *Pueblo* in the Sea of Japan. Despite a brief thaw in the cold war between the ROK and DPRK in the early 1970s, diplomatic relations reached a new low after a failed North Korean assassination attempt against ROK President Park Chung Hee. North Korean military exercises by their very nature were provocative. In this restive atmosphere, the probability of North Korean military action necessitated surges in Allied intelligence gathering. Even the frozen ground of winter, which better supported armor movement, might prompt requests for more collection.[3]

The military situation on the Korean Peninsula was as unpredictable as ever when INSCOM inherited the Army's aerial-intelligence mission on the DMZ in January 1977. In the same month, James E. "Jimmy" Carter, who had campaigned to withdraw U.S. ground forces from South Korea, assumed the presidency of the United States. The command's only means of aerial intelligence was the recently reactivated 146th ASA Company. The unit's GUARDRAIL IV system, on the cutting edge of collection and airborne radio direction finding (ARDF), was already considered irreplaceable by U.S. and ROK forces along the DMZ.

IOSS in South Korea

1977 was a notable year for Army intelligence units in Korea. The IOSS study called for their consolidation into multi-disciplined formations. At the top, INSCOM assumed ASA's SIGINT authority for the Army. ASA's commanding general, William I. Rolya, carried on as the first INSCOM commander. His close relationship with the IOSS planners gave him a first-hand understanding of the Army Staff's intentions in reorganizing military intelligence, which extended into the Korean theater.

INSCOM was primarily an administrative headquarters, responsible for bureaucratic and logistical control of its units in South Korea, while the J2 of United States Forces Korea (USFK) exercised operational control over them. To execute the reorganization, INSCOM established the provisional 501st Military Intelligence Group at Camp Coiner, South Korea, on 1 April 1977.

An aerial view of Field Station Korea, as it appeared in 1975, when GUARDRAIL IV arrived.

Then, in keeping with the multidisciplinary spirit of IOSS, the Eighth Army—the highest U.S. Army authority in South Korea—subordinated its various theater intelligence assets under this new group. This included units that would normally support an Army corps. Thus, in an unconventional command structure, INSCOM, through the 501st MI Group, was responsible for Army theater-level and corps-level support. In contrast to USAREUR and FORSCOM, the Eighth Army, although an Army-level headquarters, lacked enough units to make up even a complete corps. It therefore could not comply with the new doctrinal structure for intelligence prescribed in IOSS. Without the means to sustain an organic corps-level intelligence group, USFK relied on INSCOM to supply the Army component of their tactical intelligence support.

One of the three ADVENTURER sites.

Nearing the other end of this command chain, the 146th ASA Company served directly under U.S. Army Field Station Korea at Camp Humphreys near Pyong Taek, which in turn was directly subordinate to the 501st MI Group. In practice, this arrangement called for much of the information collected by the 146th ASA Company to feed through Field Station Korea as a conduit to the J2's staff at USFK headquarters. Regarding aviation, this relationship proved beneficial; INSCOM's staff of former ASA officers, who had managed SEMA assets since the Vietnam War, possessed highly specific qualifications to support a GUARDRAIL asset.

Serving the 501st MI Group, Field Station Korea had an uncommon layout among complexes of its type. In addition to the main site at its headquarters, the field station operated the ADVENTURER System, which consisted of three fixed border sites along the DMZ. Each site was remotely tuned and controlled from the headquarters through a microwave relay system. From their locations along the two feasible avenues of a North Korean advance—the Kaesong-Munsan approach in the west and the Chorwon approach in the center of the DMZ—operators in the field station monitored signal activity

RU-21Hs at Moffat Naval Air Station before their delivery to the 146th ASA Company.

for indications and warnings of "impending hostilities." In planning Field Station Korea, resource-conscious system designers used the ADVENTURER sites as less-than-perfect substitutes for the mobile relays used by field stations in Europe. The mostly mountainous terrain of Korea, however, obstructed the signal reception of these fixed sites. The introduction of GUARDRAIL IV gave Field Station Korea what became known as AIRBORNE ADVENTURER—a term used early in its development—a welcome SIGINT tool in this less-than-predictable signal environment.

The RU-21H GUARDRAIL IV, the first GUARDRAIL system to enter service in South Korea.

The Way to Fly

For the 146th ASA Company itself, the change from ASA to INSCOM had no effect on its military mission, which was to provide intelligence to USFK tactical commanders through airborne intercept and radio direction finding, along with ground-based analysis, processing, and reporting. The priorities of GUARDRAIL in Korea were specifically to provide the essential elements of information (mainly indications and warnings) needed by the commanding general, USFK, as tasked through his J2. Tactical MI units and other producers of intelligence were the primary consumers of GUARDRAIL IV reports. Concurrently, GUARDRAIL IV supported the Peacetime Aerial Reconnaissance Program (PARPRO) in Korea. The program provided the Joint Chiefs of Staff (JCS) with the overall means to coordinate, manage, and monitor sensitive aerial reconnaissance and surveillance missions of the Army, Navy, and Air Force worldwide.

The 146th ASA Company's original flight operations area at K-2 Airbase, Taegu, South Korea.

The company conducted aerial operations out of K-2 Air Base at Taegu. Six RU-21H aircraft flew from this location into flight patterns, south of Seoul, parallel to the DMZ. GUARDRAIL IV generally flew two daily missions, each lasting four hours. Continuous coverage was reserved for a crisis.[4] Mission flights usually required two aircraft. A single RU-21H could take direction-finding bearings with less accuracy. At times of high alert, three aircraft flew at the same time to increase collection and offer more precise fixes.

Typically, two aircraft, acting on the same direction-finding command, interacted with the IPF, which performed the calculations of triangulation to gain fixes on the target transmitters. Sometimes equipment failure prevented connectivity. In these cases, the copilot often reestablished the link in flight by leaving his position and adjusting the controls of the sensor equipment. Using his headset, he would ask an IPF technician on the ground, "which button do you want me to press?" If his attempt failed, the airplane had to return and recreate the link at the airfield.

The aircraft flew on specific paths, often through restricted airspace, roughly parallel to the DMZ, called "tracks." It took thirty to forty-five minutes to achieve altitude and reach the track from

The GUARDRAIL IV patch as worn on the aviators' flight suits.

Planting the sign in front of the Headquarters Building signified the 146th ASA Company's new home at Taegu Airbase in 1975.

the runway. GUARDRAIL platforms did not need to fly in a certain direction to pick up a signal, but proceeding along these designated tracks optimized signal monitoring in a specific geographic area of activity. The pilots synchronized their maneuvers by making simultaneous turns westbound or eastbound, sometimes resembling a choreographed dance, always mindful of the optimal geometric pattern to ascertain direction-finding locations. Their objective was an arrangement of track symmetry to have a reasonable expectation of achieving reliable measurements and "inter-hearability between the platforms," as explained in the jargon of the IPF personnel.

Navigation aids, mainly transmitting beacons on the ground, were placed according to calculated points on a map. A GUARDRAIL pilot knew his position relative to a beacon and used distance measuring equipment to determine his absolute location. Each navigation aid emitted a homing signal. When he reached the first one, he headed for the next in a series. Each beacon represented a plot on the map, and the connection of plots was a track.

Unlike the systems that characterized the ARDF effort of Vietnam, GUARDRAIL collection antennae on the RU-21H were omnidirectional. Thus, the airplane never radically changed its course to find a signal null; instead, operators could establish a line bearing from the aircraft to the target transmitter based on the trajectory angle relative to the signal's emanation.

Perhaps more than other GUARDRAIL units, the 146th ASA Company went to great lengths to make the interaction between pilot and operator as dynamic as possible. Tracks required modification

RU-21H GUARDRAIL IV covers a track over South Korea.

to increase signal amplitude, and there were specific geographic areas of activity that J2, USFK, wanted to monitor with greater attention, which invariably required some deviation from the flight plan. A secure voice communication link between the IPF and the airplanes was all-important to maintain regular feedback, so that aviators could determine how their flying affected the mission. On the ground, aviators and signal operations personnel had informal meetings at least once a week. Their regular involvement ensured that all participants had the same mission perspective. Through these practices, the pilots knew how to modify tracks with little explanation from the IPF operators, saving valuable operational time. As Chief Warrant Officer 2 Michael Bunty, the IPF commander at this time, commented, "the quality of communication and cohesiveness was of the first order; it was positively excellent."[5]

For the aviators, the well-known inadequate heating system of the RU-21 made long flights at high altitudes not only uncomfortable but harmful. A normal mission profile consisted of a four to five-hour flight at altitudes above 20,000 feet. The aviator breathed oxygen from a mask and tank, but the unpressurized cabin at low temperatures sometimes gave him altitude-induced decompression sickness with bends-like symptoms. The Army Flight Surgeon eventually introduced a preventative measure by prescribing the breathing of oxygen one-hour before and after a flight, which effectively eliminated the problem along with other pains in the limbs. Yet, the fatigue that came from flying on oxygen for long periods of time lingered, and strain on the

The "sitting ducks" patch was commonly worn by GUARDRAIL aviators flying over West Germany, but those who flew over South Korea sometimes used the image and certainly shared the sense of vulnerability.

body remained harmful. By the time a pilot completed pre-breathing and post-breathing, a flight could last as long as seven hours. Flying such missions on a continual, daily basis tested the limits of physical endurance.[6]

Perhaps of greater concern, aviators were well aware that the North Koreans could monitor their flights. As missions progressed through the years, tracks moved closer to the DMZ, and the aircraft became more vulnerable to surface-to-air and air-to-air missiles from the North. In 1978, the installation of AN/ALR-46 Radar Homing and Warning Systems on the RU-21H provided aviators with the ability to detect targeting radar, but their ability to react was limited. A few years later, the introduction of chaff—numerous small, releasable strips of aluminum, used to confuse radar—improved countermeasures, but without speed and maneuverability, GUARDRAIL aircraft were certainly a tempting target for an act of North Korean provocation. Aviators sometimes illustrated their point by wearing the informal "sitting ducks" GUARDRAIL patch on their flight suits. Nevertheless, every aviator accepted the potential for an incident when he flew and left any notions of apprehension on the ground before takeoff. Even though stress levels were high, pilots ofttimes found their own ways of lowering them through local recreational distractions, such as either a short walk to "the White House," the barracks canteen, or a long walk to the local village, called "the Vill."[7]

A view of the typical GUARDRAIL IPF vans with datalink antenna.

On the Ground: The Integrated Processing Facility

It was at Camp Humphreys, near Field Station Korea, that a detachment from the 146th ASA Company ran the IPF—the nerve center of the GUARDRAIL IV operation. Inside its two mobile trailers, called sea-land vans, each forty feet long, the equipment operators remotely manipulated the receivers and direction-finding sensors aboard the aircraft to collect, decrypt, and disseminate SIGINT. A computer directed raw data from the aircraft to one of eight operators' positions. Manned by a linguist, each one had voice intercept and direction-finding capabilities on a time-shared basis. In addition to operators and a direction-finding analyst, the IPF had four positions for three transcribers and the tactical commander of operators. The chief of the IPF sat at a collection position to assess the target environment, or he would move to the engineering position to test equipment.[8]

Mostly staff sergeants or technical specialists, IPF operators were handpicked. They were usually

132

The GUARDRAIL IV IPF operations and support NCOs in 1977. Crouching in front from left to right: SGT Fox, Mission Supervisor; SSG Preshoot, NCO in Charge of GUARDRAIL Operations; SGT Rudd, Operator Supervisor; SSG Dearth, Mission Supervisor. Back Row from left to right: SSG Moore, Operator Supervisor; SGT Bohner, Mission Supervisor; SSG Hadaway, Intelligence Analyst; SSG Poland, IPF Maintenance; SSG Spiegelberg, IPF Maintenance; SSG Gage, Mission Supervisor; SFC Anderson, Communications and Electronics Maintenance (Taegu); SFC Meade, NCO in charge of IPF Maintenance.

regular SIGINT operators or linguists, because there was no specific job category for those who worked in an IPF. When asked to account for USFK's praise of GUARDRAIL, Bunty attributed mission success to his personnel: "They were great people and I can't underemphasize that in a twenty-year career you may have the good fortune to be assigned to one or perhaps two peak organizations. The two GUARDRAIL assignments that I had in Korea were in that category. They were the best of the best." Subsequently, the chain of command never hesitated to approve decorations for these soldiers.[9]

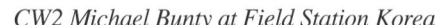
CW2 Michael Bunty at Field Station Korea.

Management of the IPF required attention to a multitude of activities. To the crew, a GUARDRAIL mission might have seemed like an orchestral performance. Success meant meticulous coordination. Preparations started two-and-a-half to three hours before takeoff. Each link required careful preflight adjustments in both the IPF and the airplane. Personnel checked all the command and data radios, performed built-in tests, and ensured the cryptologic functions. Meanwhile, the mission supervisor and senior reporters translated the general tasking from J2, USFK, into specific assignments for each operator position. After takeoff, the IPF had no contact with the aircraft until thirty minutes into the flight. A miscalculation or coordinating error would likely lead to an aborted mission. Still, such failures were a rarity.

In addition to providing administrative support, Field Station Korea normally managed the communication of operational tasking between the IPF and the J2, USFK. The field station thereby received the IPF's SIGINT products and raw data from which follow-up reports based on transcriptions were issued.[10] It also functioned as the SIGINT Collection Management Authority for GUARDRAIL activities in South Korea and kept the IPF informed of activity in the larger COMINT environment. Indeed, interaction between the IPF and the field station occurred on a daily, if not hourly, basis.

As GUARDRAIL was a tactical asset, the IPF had direct communication with line units. Through the AN/TSC-87 Tactical Commander's Terminal, encrypted reports routinely went to the headquarters of the 2d Infantry Division, I Corps, the Eighth Army, and the 1st ROK Army, all having connecting terminals. With the press of a button, the IPF could transmit a tactical report via the GUARDRAIL airplane, facilitated by an HYL-4, an in-out relay—coming in on one frequency and going out on another—to intended recipients. The receiving units had their own analysts in all-source centers to review the resulting printouts. The network of terminals also facilitated secure voice communication when more interaction was necessary.[11]

Data coming from the IPF to the field station was never in short supply: the first three months of 1977 alone yielded 2,000 intercepts. GUARDRAIL IV provided a much deeper look, beyond the forward deployed units north of the DMZ, into second echelon corps. To keep up with this heavy inflow of data, the IPF was ever expanding. During the first quarter of 1977, for instance, two more Tactical Commander's Terminals were installed for all-source intelligence dissemination. Engineers and technicians introduced a secure network to link all SIGINT systems, which improved information sharing. The Automated Switching Center was upgraded to relay defense special security traffic as well as general traffic.[12]

The demand for indications-and-warnings coverage from the J2, USFK, was unpredictable, and success often unexpectedly led to more missions as good intelligence prompted more questions. Soldiers had to arrive at the IPF with a good sense of humor about the operational pace. Bunty could recall the same comment from many of his operators after a long day: "Chief, I don't get it: the better we do, the more we have to work."[13]

Chronic manpower shortages aggravated the problem: three of the IPF's eight necessary positions were vacant during the last months of 1976. Consequently, to keep up with the standard schedule of two missions a day, the same crews had to prepare and monitor both, which left little time for rest. Additionally, they were required to maintain an alert posture in which systems had to be running and airborne within two hours of notification. On top of the usual challenges, the IPF teams reflexively prepared for extra missions during exercises, knowing well that Allied ground and naval activity invariably precipitated North Korean saber rattling. This in turn was yet another reason for the J2, USFK, to increase GUARDRAIL coverage.[14]

During surges, usually three missions per day, extreme sleep deprivation became its own test of limitation. When time permitted, off-duty IPF personnel converted a nearby trailer for spare parts into a rest area by removing interior shelves and racks and placing cots in the resulting open space. In its new configuration, the van offered a "crash pad" for sleep-deprived operators to gain two or three hours of rest while remaining available at a moment's notice. In fact, it proved indispensable during the "tree trimming incident," a particularly volatile occurrence for the USFK commanders, who were mindful of any political aggravation. In August 1976, at the height of tensions, while U.S. and ROK forces prepared a response to the North Korean provocation, the 146th ASA Company logged in as many hours as it could keep airplanes flying. On alert for ten days, GUARDRAIL flew dual missions around the clock, even after the opposing parties reconciled.[15]

In addition to perseverance, working in the IPF required patience. This virtue was especially necessary when superiors failed to grasp the capabilities and limitations of GUARDRAIL IV and pushed back against those who dampened their expectations. One such misunderstanding occurred when USFK initiated an effort in the late 1970s to detect North Korean tunneling underneath the DMZ. American experts discovered that active North Korean drills emit a sound wave at a frequency less than 100 hertz. Consequently, the J2 staff ordered the 146th ASA Company to identify and locate the drill signal. The problem was that GUARDRAIL IV had no equipment to pick up sound waves or any frequency below twenty-thousand hertz. In fact, the frequency was not even close to GUARDRAIL's lower receiving limits.

Despite Bunty's explanation for why this undertaking was impossible, the J2 representative remained adamant that the mission should continue as planned. GUARDRAIL, therefore, complied and collected signals in its range across the DMZ to make the best use of time and resources while in the air. Observing negative results after a few drill-hunting missions, the J2 staff member learned that determining mission feasibility before insisting on its execution was a better approach to tasking.

The Maintenance Problem

The aircraft were the backbone of GUARDRAIL IV operations. During fiscal year 1977, the six RU-21Hs performed 800 missions and exceeded 3,000 flight hours. In addition, the company flew a U-21A for another 1,000 hours to train new aviators. Visitors commented on the ragged appearance of the aircraft, and maintenance personnel were hard pressed to remember when any were unattended in their hangars. During intense moments, all available aircraft were in operation at one time, and some remained in the air for so long that pilots routinely declared fuel emergencies. Following one such declared emergency, the maintenance crew was astonished to discover a dry fuel tank; the pilot had only lingering fumes to thank for a safe landing. To make matters worse, the aircraft had to fly at near maximum gross weight and at maximum power for these long stretches of time. Moreover, due to their specialized logistical requirements, GUARDRAIL units were always overburdened to manage

An RU-21H GUARDRAIL IV in the maintenance bay.

aviation component lifecycles and the mechanics' tour-of-duty rotations.[16]

The GUARDRAIL mission had become vital to USFK, and having only six aerial platforms, the personnel of the 146th ASA Company were challenged with limited resources and heavy demands. The failure of an RU-21H engine on one particular mission exemplified the complex resource-demand relationship. When the aircraft lost power and went into single-engine mode, the aviators proceeded to the closest landing field at Osan Air Base. While the airplane was circling for descent, the staffs of the 146th ASA Company and Field Station Korea were already on the telephone, searching for a replacement, because the specifications of an RU-21H engine required testing at high tolerance to ensure that it had enough power to handle the GUARDRAIL IV payload. Experience had also taught them that spare aircraft parts did not always reach their intended destinations. That is, a part, marked U-21, meant for the 146th ASA Company, sometimes ended up on another airplane of the same model to satisfy the transportation needs of high-ranking officers.

In this particular case, such an undesired outcome had already occurred. A spare engine for an RU-21H had been intercepted on the supply line, placed in stocks, and later installed on a U-21, used to transport General Richard G. Stillwell, commander-in-chief of USFK and Combined Forces Command in South Korea. When General Stillwell was apprised of this detriment to GUARDRAIL operations, however, he immediately ordered his aircraft with the nonstandard engine flown to Osan Air Base for transplant to the inoperable RU-21H.[17]

Malfunctions in GUARDRAIL IV were part of the cost of operations. It was a system of systems, both delicate and highly sophisticated. If the slightest connection was made improperly, then reporting from the IPF would fail. GUARDRAIL components, from cathode ray tubes to power cords, were specially designed and not stocked in the standard issue of the Eighth Army. The men who repaired the systems, from onsite shops to the base depot, improvised at all levels of difficulty on a daily basis. For example, specialized circuit cards in IPF equipment wore out faster than the depot replacement cycle could accommodate. To compensate for the shortage of this specialty item, maintenance personnel had to put away their handbooks and devise their own system of salvage and fabrication. Another example was the heavy use of ARC-51 command aviation radios in the IPF, which caused frequent circuit burnouts and almost always incinerated two inches of their connecting cable outside the transceiver. To avoid the arduous process of replacing the cable and its peculiar connector pins, causing long periods of mission downtime, maintenance personnel simply extended the length of cord. The extra cable was then easy to splice, which allowed for quick reconnections. An IPF supervisor was prudent to keep a 33S maintenance specialist present at all times during a mission.[18]

Electrical sparks and burns were commonplace in the IPF, making explosions inevitable. Maintenance personnel were always watchful of surges coming from the unpredictable Korean power grid, but burns could result from numerous different causes. In one case, the arc guard on a power connector cable failed, causing one of its sleeves, containing magnesium, to burn. Supervising the IPF at that time, Bunty described the resulting electrical fire: "It was like the 4th of July. So many sparks flew. The sleeve completely disintegrated. And the spray of molten connector pieces burned some of the guy ropes supporting the antennas. Antennas were falling like trees!"[19]

From a technical standpoint, ESL had designed an impressive system, but the designers never considered the extreme environmental conditions in Korea. Summers were extremely hot and humid.

Winters were severely cold and dry. IPF air conditioners, which typically broke down during the summer, required removal and transport to a depot for repair. Operators and analysts were the only manpower available to move the heavy and cumbersome machines. Without air conditioning, the humidity made the plywood floor swell and buckle. Then, floor tiles would come loose. Improvised drain holes were necessary to prevent large puddles of water from expanding because of condensation. While these problems required careful attention on a regular basis, delaying a mission was unacceptable.

Although the obstacles in front of the 146th ASA Company were formidable, they were not insurmountable. For direct technical electronic support, ESL kept dedicated representatives at Field Station Korea to handle any contingency. ESL experts, such as Michael Britz, who had a reputation for being a bulldog on a problem until it was solved, ensured that the IPF was in constant working order and properly upgraded. John McMains, a Stanford graduate and qualified astronaut, lent the highest level of technical expertise to the GUARDRAIL aviation systems. ESL personnel reinforced the expectation that the 146th ASA Company could always meet the needs of USFK.[20]

Despite the difficulties of supporting a unit described as being at the end of the supply chain and on the other side of the international dateline, INSCOM headquarters at Arlington Hall was well aware of the company's difficulties and always remained diligent in providing personnel, money, equipment, and policy guidance. To oversee aviation assets, INSCOM's Deputy Chief of Staff for Operations (DCSOPS) relied on the Aviation Safety and Standards Program. The executive agent of the program was the INSCOM Aviation Section, headed by the INSCOM Aviation Officer (originally a major and later a lieutenant colonel). He ensured that INSCOM aviation assets (including support aircraft at various field stations) complied with the standards and administrative requirements of the Department of the Army and the command.

As part of a vast intelligence organization, INSCOM personnel understood that the 146th ASA Company's critical mission required an aggressive approach to its care and feeding. From that standpoint, when an airframe or the IPF needed parts or repairs, the Deputy Chief of Staff for Logistics (DCSLOG) would waste no time in responding. For this reason, specialized parts and regular supplies arrived quickly and often in greater quantities than requested to offset the difficulties in one of the most isolated Army theaters.[21]

Much of INSCOM's logistical and technical success was due to a close working relationship

Then BG Rolya awards the Legion of Merit to CW3 Alan Lindley at Arlington Hall Station in February 1976.

between DCSLOG Chief Warrant Officer 3 Alan L. Lindley and the staff of the 146th ASA Company. A logistician with expertise in intelligence technologies as well as supply, Lindley had worked at SIGINT sites in South Korea since 1957 and had a good understanding of the support that a unit needed in that area of the world. He was also familiar with the threat environment as it related to the objectives of the company. Indeed, he would go on to become one of the very few logistics experts to enter the Military Intelligence Hall of Fame at Fort Huachuca, Arizona. Lindley and his team also ensured that new equipment both reached the unit and achieved mission functionality. Most important, he had in-depth experience with SEMA maintenance and logistics from his service in the 138th Aviation Company in Vietnam. The 146th ASA Company and Field Station Korea came to rely on INSCOM through Lindley for the upkeep of their systems. According to Bunty, a shortage was easily rectified with a routine call to Lindley "to get a spare or any type of supply."[22]

Making the System Better

Only months after its implementation, GUARDRAIL IV had proven itself to Field Station Korea, USFK, and the Eighth Army, but there was always room for technical and doctrinal improvement. At issue during 1977 was a modification of its flight path. For their first two years of operation, GUARDRAIL platforms flew along one of six tracks south of Seoul. The main drawbacks to this flight path were the great distances from the DMZ and electromagnetic interference from the bustling metropolis of the ROK capital.

Moving the tracks north to fly between Seoul and the DMZ was an obvious improvement to gain better intelligence. Flying closer to North Korea would extend GUARDRAIL's radio horizon and reception, and any position north of Seoul eliminated significant radio frequency interference. Even so, the benefits were offset by the aircrafts' greater vulnerability when flying in closer proximity to the DMZ. The JCS, cautious of accepting greater risks in peacetime, resisted any movement that might make the pilots and aircraft larger in the gun sights of the volatile regime to the north. On the other hand, the J2s of USFK and the U.S. Pacific Command (PACOM) argued that GUARDRAIL was a tactical asset and not designed to operate as "a long distance, standoff platform." In compromise, JCS agreed on testing the proposed tracks for a period of ninety days to determine if the benefits really outweighed the added risk.[23]

Initiating tests in July 1977, the RU-21Hs flew both sets of tracks with an equal number of missions to make a comparison. Regarding collection volume and direction-finding fixes, the results overwhelmingly favored using the northern tracks. Yet, amid warnings against placing GUARDRAIL at greater risk, JCS ordered an extension of the ninety-day trial. Continuation, however, only provided more confirmation that closer tracks yielded greatly improved reception and made the risks appear smaller. Among the aviators and company staff, the debate was already settled. If they were to risk their lives collecting data, they wanted to make the most out of each flight. The interested parties, therefore, agreed to adjust their flight patterns along the newly proposed tracks.[24]

Perhaps the key to the unit's success was support from above, best characterized by a motto that the first commanding general of INSCOM, Major General William I. Rolya, often expressed to his subordinates: "mission first, people always."[25] He firmly believed that if a commander takes care of his people, they will take care of the mission. His motto also reflected INSCOM's commitment to support the company's mission in Korea. Commanding the IPF, Bunty remembered these words and their impact on his unit when put into practice: "I found a lot of truth in that statement. Major General Rolya practiced what he preached when he said this. The support that we received from INSCOM was proof. We got the support and the personnel that we needed. Then he got out of our way and let us execute the mission."[26]

The early years of GUARDRAIL in South Korea proved that SEMA systems were not only effective but capable of adaptation. The troops of the 146th ASA Company and Field Station Korea established a precedent that GUARDRAIL would be a living system, receptive to improvement, whether it occurred in the laboratory or in the field, confirmed by its continued indispensability to USFK. In testament, the 146th ASA Company (Aviation) (GUARDRAIL IV) was nominated in 1977 by the Army Aviation Association of America for the "Outstanding Aviation Unit Award" for providing intelligence "under extremely demanding conditions."[27] At the start of IOSS implementation, the GUARDRAIL IV system, operational for only a year, proved the equal to its seasoned European counterpart, GUARDRAIL IIA. More important to the Army, however, both systems proved the value of airborne SIGINT in watching over the static yet volatile lines of demarcation that defined the Cold War.

By 1978, the North Korean Army
had roughly seven-hundred maneuver battalions,
nearly twice the number in previous intelligence estimates
and double the size of ROK forces. Perhaps more sobering,
the North had half the population of the South but almost twice the army.
In fact, according to new data, the DPRK had more men under arms
in proportion to its population than any other nation in the world.—

CHAPTER FIVE:
Predicament on the Korean Peninsula

As airborne SIGINT on the Korean Peninsula matured, USFK and INSCOM determined that the time was right to move towards the Army intelligence staff's long-term objective to unify small units of a single-intelligence discipline into those of a larger, more cohesive, multidisciplinary character. For MI aviation, the process called for grouping companies and detachments, each using one distinct type of sensor, into battalions for better management of aviation assets and greater unity of effort.

In South Korea, the task, however simple on paper, could not be accomplished in a day or even in a year. The restructuring plan required the introduction of new staff positions and cooperation with different chains of command as well as with consumers of aerial intelligence. More important, any structural change had to occur without any lapse in operational output. For planners, the foremost problem was accounting for the unexpected on the other side of the DMZ, which could come in many forms. As reorganization progressed, the DPRK lived up to pessimistic expectations by presenting a major military threat with grave political repercussions. For this reason, the process of consolidating aerial-intelligence units had to be incremental and gradual.

An Inconvenient Discovery

In the late 1970s, relations between the governments of the ROK and DPRK had reached a new low. Between Washington and Seoul, an American diplomatic effort had, with great effort, succeeded in persuading the ROK government to abandon its nascent nuclear research program. Meanwhile, President Jimmy Carter was resolute in his campaign promise to withdraw all U.S. land forces from the Korean Peninsula. His proposed U.S. withdrawal had also long been DPRK President Kim Il Sung's goal. In contrast to Carter's hopes for a lasting peace, Kim saw such a move as an opportunity to unite the peninsula under his leadership either through diplomatic coercion or military invasion. Probably Kim's greatest concern was the rising South Korean economy, which had only recently surpassed that of the North in production. For ROK president, Park Chung Hee, the rise in productivity presented a long-awaited political opening to double defense expenditures. Unknown to the U.S.-ROK alliance, a massive buildup of North Korean military formations along the DMZ had been underway since the early 1970s. For the North Korean military supreme command, the optimal moment for a successful reunification by force was approaching, but if the ROK were to conduct a similar buildup, opportunity would be fleeting.

The North Korean buildup had gone unnoticed until John H.

John H. Armstrong (left) receives the Exceptional Civilian Service Award from Secretary of the Army Clifford Alexander. Also present is Army Assistant Chief of Staff for Intelligence MG Edmund Thompson. ASA, later INSCOM, headquarters, Arlington Hall Station, in Arlington, Virginia.

Armstrong, an intelligence analyst, who would later work for INSCOM's Intelligence Threat and Analysis Center (ITAC), reached a surprising conclusion while examining aerial photographs of DPRK forces in 1975. He became suspicious after counting many more tanks in a specific area than earlier reports had indicated. Further investigation over a few weeks revealed the addition of an entirely new tank division (270 tanks and 100 armored personnel carriers) in a valley only fifty miles from the DMZ. In light of Armstrong's alarming findings, ITAC initiated a large-scale intelligence study over the next three years to determine conclusively the extent of a substantial North Korean force increase along the border.[1]

ITAC was distinctive among INSCOM's major subordinate commands. Collocated with the INSCOM headquarters at Arlington Hall Station, this analytical center had only recently come into existence on 1 October 1977.[†] Like many of INSCOM's other subordinate units, ITAC was the result

† ITAC was established on 1 October 1977 as an interim organization and was not established permanently until 1 January 1978.

The ITAC production center at the Washington Navy Yard in Washington, DC.

of an IOSS consolidation of six independently functioning intelligence production organizations (primarily serving under the Army Assistant Chief of Staff for Intelligence) into a singular entity to reduce overhead supervisory, administrative, and logistical support positions and personnel. ITAC's imagery section, the Imagery Intelligence Production Division, came from one of these six organizations. Previously, this division had been the Imagery Interpretation Center at Fort Meade, Maryland, and before that, the Photographic Interpretation Center at Fort Holabird, Maryland. Mainly, it produced reports informed by sensors mounted on a variety of platforms, from satellites to OV-1 Mohawk aircraft.[2] Armstrong's initial observations originated from this organization when it had been the Imagery Interpretation Center.

Falling under the Imagery Intelligence Production Division after the reorganization and later renamed the Capabilities and Readiness Division, Armstrong had to assemble a dedicated team to prepare a detailed report on the North Korean build-up. Thirty-four expert analysts and image interpreters were brought to ITAC on temporary duty assignments from units of INSCOM, FORSCOM, U.S. Army Training and Doctrine Command, USAREUR, and the Eighth Army. This collaboration was collectively known as the North Korea Special Studies Team, which consisted of elements dedicated to IMINT, SIGINT, and human intelligence. Politicians and military personnel who questioned the Carter administration's plan to withdraw troops from Korea were deeply concerned over Armstrong's initial findings and eagerly awaited the issuance of his final report. Intelligence collection on the peninsula, therefore, had become a component of a heated political debate in Washington, DC. [3]

Watch over the DMZ

Imagery had been essential to constructing the intelligence picture, not only to inform national political debates but also to correct tactical misperceptions. Although satellites provided the most

revealing views, nothing could replace the great volume of imagery collected by aerial reconnaissance and surveillance. Furthermore, satellites were hindered by overcast weather and nighttime conditions, but the OV-1D Mohawk, using IMINT cameras or side-looking radar, was effective at any time. As the threat appeared greater, more collection was needed to verify the enemy's posture and perhaps even to anticipate an attack, which compelled the Joint Staff to authorize an expansion of the IMINT mission in Korea. For

An aerial view of Camp Humphreys Airfield (Pyong Taek). By this time, the 146th ASA Company had transferred its GUARDRAIL IV aircraft from Taegu to this airfield.

USFK and the Eighth Army, any such increase would require action from one of the heavy movers of airborne imagery in Korea, the 704th Military Intelligence Detachment (Aerial Surveillance), commonly known as the 704th MIDAS, under the 19th Aviation Battalion.

Activated on 25 September 1976 at K-16 Air Force Base, in Songnam (just south of Seoul), the 704th MI Detachment had originally been a counterintelligence unit in South Korea and Vietnam. In its new role and configuration, however, the unit had an entirely different mission: to conduct, "both day and night under Visual Flight Rules or Instrument Meteorological Conditions Side-Looking Airborne Radar (SLAR) aerial surveillance." Regarding operational duties, the 704th MIDAS laid claim to a relevant heritage beginning when a few RL-23D Seminoles equipped with the AN/APQ-86

Group photograph of the 704th MIDAS in 1978.

SLAR system began nighttime flights along the DMZ in 1961. Flying in the 7th Aviation Company, 7th Infantry Division, the RL-23Ds were based at an Army airfield located on Yeouido Island in the Han River, south of Seoul. Technical complications ended this early SLAR mission within one year.

The first OV-1A Mohawks arrived in Korea in October 1963 for aerial observation. They were part of the Aerial Surveillance and Target Acquisition (ASTA) Platoon, 55th Aviation Company, 52d Aviation Battalion. In November 1964, six SLAR-equipped OV-1Bs arrived to assume the mission formerly conducted by the RL-23Ds. Flying as part of 2d ASTA Platoon, 2d Infantry Division, these Mohawks were also based on Yeouido Island. In May 1970, the OV-1B unit was redesignated as the 6th Aviation Platoon (Aerial Surveillance), assigned to the 55th Aviation Company, 17th Aviation Group.[4]

In April 1971, the platoon moved to Seoul Air Force Base in support of theater and national-level consumers. Disbanded in 1976, the platoon's assets including six newly arrived OV-1Ds, which assumed the mission of all OV-1As, Bs, and Cs previously flying in South Korea, formed the nucleus of the newly activated 704th MIDAS under the 19th Aviation Battalion. The creation of this

LTC William B. Guild, Commander of Field Station Korea, exchanges a guidon with CPT Mark L. Kogle, Commander of the 704th MIDAS.

detachment effectively consolidated all airborne-IMINT functions of the Army in South Korea into one mission and one unit.[5]

The first nine months of the detachment's existence were erratic: it had been attached to three different headquarters, had two detachment commanders, relocated to a new operating facility—Camp Humphreys Army Airfield (Pyong Taek)—and changed billeting four times. As the detachment personnel were to discover, however, what seemed like an uncertain existence was part of the preparation for a much larger consolidation. Thus, on 1 July 1977, the 704th MIDAS was transferred directly to U.S. Army Field Station Korea, which also had command over the 146th ASA Company. The transfer thereby completed the wholesale consolidation of Army aerial-intelligence assets in South Korea under the 501st MI Group, a major subordinate command of INSCOM.[6] Finally on 1 November 1978, the 146th ASA Company assumed direct authority over the detachment.

The OV-1D—the culmination of Mohawk development—had become indispensable to the Army in South Korea. Of these six aircraft in the 704th MIDAS, one was equipped with dual

An OV-1D Mohawk of the 704th MIDAS flies a routine mission.

controls for training; the other five were available for surveillance with cameras—capable of using three different photographic systems—and either SLAR or Infrared (IR) detectors. (Payload capacity was not large enough to carry both SLAR and IR detectors.) Already known for its durability and resilience, the OV-1D proved a versatile and capable aerial-intelligence platform. Its various imaging systems, mounted underneath and on both sides of the aerial platform, produced both

More than a patch, the "Mohawk" image might appear in any location where the 704th MIDAS resided.

The "Spectre" OV-1 image was closely associated with unit identity.

Soldiers of the 704th MIDAS stand in formation as OV-1Ds fly overhead during a ceremony.

photographic film and televised imagery of the terrain and activity ahead. Its IR sensors detected heat from campfires and even vehicle engines. Moreover, unusual activity that registered on these sensors prompted and informed other surveillance systems in the 501st MI Group.[7]

With the Mohawk's proven capabilities, the pilots and crew of the 704th MIDAS had the utmost confidence in their ability to monitor the DMZ. In South Korea, the OV-1D pilots trained for two types of intelligence missions: "standoff" and "penetration." In standoff missions, the aerial platform flew over friendly terrain (yet within range of North Korean surface-to-air missiles), employing SLAR, IR, and regular photography to observe enemy positions. Penetration missions were far more dangerous, requiring flights deep into enemy territory at very low altitudes to avoid detection. The personnel of the 704th MIDAS prepared for both, but unless the peninsula erupted in war, USFK prohibited penetration missions.[8]

An OV-1D Mohawk on the flight line features a frontal view of the SLAR system.

In the "standoff" mission posture, SLAR was the most important sensor. It had been in service since 1957 in various peacetime and combat functions, including mapping and geology. In fact, the 704th MIDAS based its operational cover story on low altitude terrain sketching and profile mapping in support of landscape analysis. SLAR derived its effectiveness from the concept of detecting targets by transmitting a narrow beam of electromagnetic energy in pulses, at a relatively low angle toward the earth's surface. Reflected radar emissions detected moving vehicles (known as moving target indicator or MTI capability) in line of sight by measuring the Doppler shift in the returning radar waves. Most important, the system allowed forward units to monitor vehicular traffic patterns across the DMZ, including those moving as slowly as 1.5 miles per hour. OV-1Ds of the late 1970s used the AN/APS-94D SLAR, which emitted and received radar signals at an effective range of one-hundred kilometers on level terrain. Processed into visual images, the feedback revealed the size, composition, and incident angles of targets, a vast improvement over photographic images by virtue of SLAR's availability day and night in all weather conditions.[9]

USFK and the Eighth Army used the SLAR mission—codenamed BADGE KEEPER—to monitor territory mainly as an early warning indicator of a mobilization across the DMZ. Because the North Korean nightly curfew limited traffic exclusively to military purposes after dark, the 704th MIDAS employed these systems primarily between the hours of 2000 to 0400, during times of known minimal civilian activity, thus eliminating interference from farming and utility vehicles. In that way, SLAR worked well to detect unusual vehicular activity under the cover of night, including blackouts, when other sensors were unavailable. Image interpreters who worked with MTI over the years had a detailed tracking system to compare incoming data with records of regular civilian and military traffic patterns, specific to any given day of the year.

The timely dissemination and analysis of imagery data was vital to USFK. A sensor specialist (96H), often called a technical observer, usually a private or low-ranking noncommissioned officer, operated SLAR from the right side of the OV-1D cockpit and provided initial analysis of imagery from a display. Incoming sensor data was also downlinked to two ground station terminals, one at the Combined Field Army Headquarters in Uijongbu and the other in Wonju. Observing the same readout as that on the technical observer's monitor, intelligence analysts at these locations could view MTI data from their terminals. They could then report to the G2 staffs of the 2d Infantry Division and the Eighth Army, which in turn posted indications and warnings for all forces in South Korea. The recipients' downlinked view of information allowed consumers to pick up time-critical snippets of information about North Korean movement across from their respective sector as the Mohawk flew on a track parallel to the DMZ. When the aircraft returned to Camp Humphreys, technicians transmitted a mission report along with time-sensitive photographs over a secure telephone to the J2, USFK, in Seoul while sensor products were forwarded to a facility for light-table analysis and detailed reporting. Six imagery analysts worked in shifts around the clock. Their familiarity with the target area enabled them to highlight inconspicuous changes in movement patterns by plotting and comparing the grid coordinates of each MTI.[10]

As a Mohawk pilot, CPT Mark L. Kogle's flight suit displays the distinctive Mohawk patch on the right pocket.

SLAR, however, did not overshadow the continuing value of PHOTINT and daytime missions. When the North Korean Army changed doctrine to increase the distance between large artillery pieces for improved survivability, analysts of the 501st MI Group requested photographs of North Korean field artillery exercises in March and April 1978 to study the repositioning for counter-battery fire. In addition to flying fifty-five sorties per month, Captain Mark L. Kogle, the detachment commander, authorized the 704th MIDAS to expand mission tracks for "greater coverage of the DMZ and adjacent waters," resulting in a view of previously masked North Korean terrain. The resulting photographs revealed an expansion of control elements accompanied by more diversified equipment. This evidence was yet another piece of information contributing to Armstrong's dire intelligence picture.[11]

Although IMINT was driving his analysis, SIGINT provided further supporting information. The 146th ASA Company under the command of Major Harry E. Cryblskey contributed intercept data about the extreme eastern and western areas over the DMZ to inform the North Korea Special Studies Team. Throughout this process, the IPF analyzed routine communications to identify missing pieces of the military order of battle such as corps-level air defense assets. The company's final report noted a vastly enlarged deployment of forward artillery and confirmed that the North Korean army was using mockups of South Korean highways for commando training. Analysts were then able to isolate and study a large portion of its forward artillery forces. General John W. Vessey, the Commanding General of Combined Forces Command, USFK, and the Eighth Army, issued a letter of commendation to the company for its contribution during this critical period.[12]

A Disquieting Conclusion

As more information reached the North Korea Special Studies Team, the threat from the North appeared far graver than was generally known. In December 1977, Armstrong had presented his research team's preliminary findings to the Eighth Army headquarters in Seoul. Among his conclusions was information revealing the existence of at least nine previously unknown North Korean Army divisions and one brigade. At last, Vessey sensed the opening he needed to voice his resistance to the Carter administration's withdrawal program. In the following month, enough evidence was available to call for a complete intelligence reassessment of North Korean military strength from the DMZ to the Yalu River. The Department of Defense, in response, gathered experts from around the world to scrutinize all intelligence reports since the armistice and reexamine IMINT and SIGINT collected since 1969. In July 1978, Armstrong's conclusions and supporting evidence were presented in a classified briefing to senior officials in the Pentagon.[13]

His study identified every unit down to companies and noted a preponderance of forces closely emplaced along the DMZ. Estimates suggested that the DPRK had

MAJ Ted Cryblskey would later oversee the Mohawk mission in South Korea when the 146th ASA Company became a dual-disciplined unit by assuming control of the 704th MIDAS.

undertaken a steady buildup of forces since 1971-72, and that the number of tanks and artillery pieces in North Korea had been grossly underestimated. By 1978, the North Korean Army had roughly seven-hundred maneuver battalions, nearly twice the number in previous intelligence estimates and double the size of ROK forces. Perhaps more sobering, the North had half the population of the South but almost twice the army. In fact, according to new data, the DPRK had more men under arms in proportion to its population than any other nation in the world. More to the point, when the final report was released in July 1979, its central judgment not only presented evidence but also determined the DPRK's intent:

> [B]y 1969, Pyongyang began the execution of a coherent master plan, set down
> by Kim Il-song, calling for the creation of a military force capable of effecting
> national reunification of the Korean Peninsula at the time of Kim's choosing; by the
> mid-1970's, the desired force had been created; and by early 1979, the remaining
> fleshing out, training, and meticulous planning had been accomplished to such a
> degree that an offensive option was finally viable.[14]

Although Armstrong's initial briefing to the Pentagon was restricted to the level of high-ranking officials, the information was leaked to *The Army Times* and *The Washington Post* in January 1979, months before the release of the final official report. The publicity forced President Carter to realign with his cabinet members, who had already concluded that withdrawing all U.S. ground forces from Korea was imprudent. In the end, his bold initiative for force reduction was postponed indefinitely.[15]

The 146th ASA Company found itself at the forefront of a major intelligence operation that profoundly affected national as well as military policy in the Korean theater. Almost overnight, with the incorporation of the 704th MIDAS, the company gained an IMINT mission during a crucial period of reporting. Moreover, its link to INSCOM facilitated a line of communication and collaboration with ITAC, which verified an ominous revelation across the DMZ. For service in a year with many challenges, the Army Aviation Association of America bestowed the award for the Army Aviation Unit of the Year upon the 146th ASA Company. General Edward C. Meyer, Army Chief of Staff, presented the award and described the unit's performance for 1979:

I can merely tell you that in the past year the demands for intelligence and warning in Korea have been far greater than they have been in the past, not necessarily greater over the full period of time but the threat there has continued to evolve and that the capacity which this particular aviation company has been able to provide to the commander in Korea has significantly filled the intelligence and warning voids that we've not been able to get from some of the other high flying aircraft which are only provided to you in those instances when they happen to be over the particular targets.[16]

Epilogue

Since the advent of aviation, military thinkers have sought to harness its potential to serve intelligence. Not surprisingly, the U.S. Army has benefited from the enduring relationship between aviation and intelligence. In the early years of this partnership, its purview was primarily tactical, but as this new discipline matured, its capabilities diversified through technology, organization, and processes to fill greater roles. Yet, throughout its evolution in the early twentieth century, MI aviation lacked a benefactor at the higher levels of command in the Army and suffered from poor integration with other emerging intelligence disciplines. More recently, reforms have shown the way to a brighter future, but that outcome was uncertain throughout most of the Cold War. In those years, a small cadre of professionals had to improvise, economize, and remain committed.

Starting in the First World War, fixed-wing aircraft revolutionized reconnaissance and surveillance on the battlefield. Without them, impending enemy attacks were all but impossible to anticipate. Moreover, analysis of observation data provided an operational picture to the Allied theater command. Nevertheless, this new asset was not centrally managed or collectively organized. From the Second World War onward, even as the quality of aerial reconnaissance improved, the impetus to strengthen its association with the Army's intelligence structure was lacking. This precluded opportunities for information sharing and synergy as well as improvement in administrative and logistical efficiency.

Events in the Cold War, specifically in Vietnam, allowed an intelligence organization, ASA, to make a small inroad in controlling an aviation asset. Imagining the possibilities, ASA developers introduced an effective means of utilizing ARDF exclusively within their own units, starting with the 3d RRU. The 224th Aviation Battalion (RR) became its inheritor. Success made the Army leadership receptive to more ventures that linked intelligence with aviation on a larger scale, such as when Army force management rebranded Mohawk units from reconnaissance to MI. Furthermore, ASA began to implement SEMA systems, most notably GUARDRAIL, for service beyond Vietnam.

IOSS might have reversed this organizational shift if not for INSCOM's control of a single SEMA unit, the 146th ASA Company, in South Korea. Flying near the contested DMZ with both GUARDRAIL and Mohawk SLAR systems, this lonely company demonstrated the advantages of having SEMA systems supported directly by an intelligence organization. Indeed, its effectiveness became clear when INSCOM analysts in ITAC were able to verify a massive buildup of North Korean forces along the DMZ, reversing a U.S. policy of force reduction in South Korea and perhaps averting a conflict. ITAC not only consumed information from the 146th ASA Company but also directed the next stage of the unit's collection effort, proving the benefit of interaction among intelligence units within a common organizational structure.

INSCOM's relationship to the 146th ASA Company redefined the partnership between aviation and intelligence in the Army. In its formative years, MI aviation relied heavily on improvisation in a highly technical field, requiring flexibility and resourcefulness because support was not always available. Under such conditions, success was hard won, and systemization was a challenge. When aerial intelligence functioned within a contained MI-based institutional structure, all players were fully engaged and collaborated toward solutions. Moreover, encouraged after overcoming a myriad of challenges and perhaps emboldened following their Korean success, INSCOM's aviation and logistical staff elements would take the lead in developing experimental SEMA systems that supported military efforts in remote locations, such as in Central America.

INSCOM had become more than just a place for MI aviation in the Army. The command's delineated, well-established programs for research and development, acquisition, training, and implementation were capable of cultivating the full potential of aerial intelligence. Indeed, over the next three decades, INSCOM's aviation responsibilities would grow from holding a few GUARDRAIL systems in South Korea to directly running all SEMA (later called AISR) assets in the Army. Thus, this is not the epilogue to a short story but rather the prologue to one much longer.

Glossary of Acronyms

A

ACC ARDF Coordination Center

ACTIV Army Concept Team in Vietnam

AFB Air Force Base

AGE Auxiliary Ground Equipment

AISR Aerial Intelligence, Surveillance, and Reconnaissance

ARDF Airborne Radio Direction Finding

ARVN Army of the Republic of Vietnam

ASA United States Army Security Agency

ASARDA Army Security Agency Research and Development Agency

C

COMINT Communications Intelligence

D

DCSLOG Deputy Chief of Staff for Logistics

DCSOPS Deputy Chief of Staff for Operations

DMZ Demilitarized Zone

DPRK Democratic People's Republic of Korea

E

EAC Echelons Above Corps

ELINT Electronic Intelligence

ESL Electronic Systems Laboratories

EW Electronic Warfare

EWL Electronic Warfare Laboratory

F

FORSCOM United States Army Forces Command

G

G2 Army officer in charge of military intelligence on a general's staff

GAO Government Accounting Office

I

IMINT Imagery Intelligence

INSCOM United States Army Intelligence and Security Command

IOSS Intelligence Organization and Stationing Study

IPF Integrated Processing Facility

IR Infrared

IRAN Inspect and Repair As Necessary

ISR Intelligence, Surveillance, and Reconnaissance

ITAC United States Army Intelligence Threat and Analysis Center

J

J2 Officer in charge of intelligence on a joint staff

JCS Joint Chiefs of Staff

JSA Joint Security Area

M

MACV Military Assistance Command Vietnam

MDL Military Demarcation Line

MI Military Intelligence

MIBARS Military Intelligence Battalion (Air Reconnaissance Support)

MRF Mobile Relay Facility

MTI Moving Target Indication or Moving Target Indicator

N

NATO North Atlantic Treaty Organization

NSA National Security Agency

NSA/CSS National Security Agency/Central Security Service

NSG Naval Security Group

P

PACOM United States Pacific Command

PARPRO Peacetime Aerial Reconnaissance Program

PHOTINT Photographic Intelligence

PIC Photographic Interpretation Center

PSA Pacific Southwest Airlines

Q

QRC Quick Reaction Capability

R

ROK The Republic of Korea

RR Radio Research

RRU Radio Research Unit

S

S2 Officer in charge of intelligence on an Army brigade or battalion staff

SAC Strategic Air Command

SAD Special Activities Detachment

SEMA Special Electronic Mission Aircraft

SI Special Intelligence or Sensitive Information

SIGINT Signals Intelligence

SLAR Side-Looking Airborne Radar

SOCOM United States Special Operations Command

SRI Stanford Research Institute

SSA Signal Security Agency

T

TACAN Tactical Air Navigation

TRW Thompson Ramo Wooldridge

TWA Teeny Weeny Airlines

U

UHF Ultra High Frequency

UN United Nations

USASA United States Army Security Agency

USEUCOM United States European Command

USFK United States Forces Korea

USSOUTHCOM United States Southern Command

V

VHF Very High Frequency

End Notes

Chapter One

1. Rebecca Robbins Raines, *Getting the Message Through: A Branch History of the U.S. Army Signal Corps* (Washington, DC: U.S. Army Center of Military History, 1995), 128.

2. Ibid., 129.

3. Ibid., 131.

4. Juliette A. Hennessy, *The United States Army Air Arm, April 1861 to April 1917* (Washington, DC: Office of Air Force History, United States Air Force, 1958), 33; Edgar F. Raines, *Eyes of Artillery: The Origins of Modern U.S. Army Aviation in World War II* (Washington, D.C.: U.S. Army Center of Military History, 2000), 8.

5. Rebecca Robbins Raines, *Getting the Message Through*, 145.

6. Edgar F. Raines, "Corps Observation in the AEF, 1917-1918" *A Paper Prepared for Delivery at the History of Air Power Course* (Air Force History Support Office, Bolling Air Force Base, 30 July 1996), 1.

7. Maurer Maurer, *The US Air Service in World War I* (Washington, DC: Office of Air Force History, 1978), 1: 154; Raines, "Corps Observation in the AEF, 1917-1918," 10-11.

8. Howard K. Butler, *Army Air Corps Airplanes and Observation: 1935-1941* (Saint Louis, MO: Historical Office, United States Aviation Systems Command, 1990), 189.

9. Ibid., 190.

10. John Patrick Finnegan and Romana Danysh, *Military Intelligence* (Washington, DC: U.S. Army Center of Military History, 1998), 97.

11. Glenn B. Infield, *Unarmed and Unafraid: The First Complete History of the Men, Missions, Training, and Techniques of Aerial Reconnaissance* (London, The MacMillan Company, 1970), 62.

12. Brigadier General Oscar W. Koch with Robert Hays, *G2: Intelligence for Patton* (Atglen, PA: Schiffer Publishing Ltd., 1999), 90, 94.

13. As quoted in John Patrick Finnegan and Romana Danysh, *Military Intelligence* (Washington, DC: U.S. Army Center of Military History, 1998), 115.

14. Finnegan and Danysh, *Military Intelligence*, 119.

15. Ibid.

16. Ibid., 131.

17. Carlos M. Collat, "The History, the Legacy, and the Message of Army SEMA," (7 March 2005), United States Army Intelligence and Security Command Cryptologic Records Repository and Command History Office Files (hereafter cited as INSCOM Historical Files), 2.

18. Chief Warrant Officer 3 Edward Jones, "Special Electronic Mission Aircraft: Intelligence from Above," *United States Army Aviation Digest* 27, no. 4 (April 1981) : 4.

19. Ibid.

20. Danny Johnson, "Grumman OV-1 Mohawk," *On Point: The Journal of Army History*, 11, no. 2 (Fall 2005) : 13.

21. Ibid.

22. Ibid.

23. Finnegan and Danysh, *Military Intelligence*, 260; Karen Kovach, "Imagery Intelligence and the Army" (21 January 2000), INSCOM Historical Files, 1; Army Imagery Milestones, INSCOM Historical Files. See Table of Organization and Equipment 11-54D (1957).

24. Finnegan and Danysh, *Military Intelligence*, 131; Kovach, "Imagery Intelligence and the Army," 2.

25. Papers of Dennis Buley (hereafter cited as Buley Papers), "Prologue to ARDF," INSCOM Historical Files, 3. Earlier project names for this venture included FLOOR DOOR and LAND BOOM SPECIAL.

26. Ibid.

27. Ibid., 10.

28. Buley Papers, "Prologue to ARDF," 15.

29. Ibid.

Chapter Two

1. Finnegan and Danysh, *Military Intelligence*, 152.

2. Ibid.

3. James L. Gilbert, *The Most Secret War* (Washington, DC: Government Publishing Office, 2003), 4.

4. Ibid., 6.

5. James L. Gilbert, "Airborne Radio Direction Finding," in *A History of Innovation: U.S. Army Adaptation in War and Peace*, ed. Jon T. Hoffman (Washington DC: U.S. Government Publishing Office, 2009), 129-130. James Davis, one of the 10 casualties in this ambush, became known as the first fatality of the Vietnam War. He was memorialized in Vietnam with the naming of the facility of the 509th Radio Research Group as Davis Station. INSCOM Headquarters also has a memorial to his sacrifice.

6. Ibid.

7. Buley Papers, "The Beginning of ARDF," 4.

8. Gilbert, "Airborne Radio Direction Finding," 132-133; Buley Papers, "The Beginning of ARDF," 5-6; Carlos Collat, GUARDRAIL Presentation, (11 August 1991), INSCOM Historical Files, 5.

9. E. R. Johnson and Lloyd S. Jones, *American Military Transport Aircraft since 1925* (Jefferson, NC: McFarland and Company, Inc., 2013), 412-413.

10. Gilbert, "Airborne Radio Direction Finding," 132-133; Buley Papers, "The Beginning of ARDF," 6; Carlos Collat, GUARDRAIL Presentation, 5.

11. General Orders (hereafter cited as GO) 22, Headquarters, United States Department of the Army, 14 May 1963; James L. Gilbert, "Airborne Radio Direction Finding," 135.

12. Lillian Reed, "Signals Director Retires after 33 Years," *The Monmouth Message*, (8 June 1990), 10.

13. Buley Papers, "The Beginning of ARDF," 5.

14. Center for Cryptologic History, National Security Agency, *Army Security Agency Aerial Reconnaissance: Mission and Sacrifice*, Fort George G. Meade, NSA, no date, 2; *Airborne Radio Direction Finding Manual*, Headquarters, 3d Radio Research Unit, 21 August 1962, Background.

15. E. R. Johnson and Lloyd S. Jones, *American Military Transport Aircraft since 1925*, 416; 138th Military Intelligence Company (AE) History, INSCOM Historical Files.

16. Origins of the Army Security Agency and INSCOM, INSCOM Historical Files, 4; Navigation/Communications, INSCOM Historical Files.

17. Shelby L. Stanton, *US Army and Allied Ground Forces in Vietnam Order of Battle* (Washington, DC: US News Books, 1981), 236. See Table of Organization and Equipment 30-5D (1963).

18. Douglas W. Bonnet, *The Sentinel and the Shooter* (Livermore, CA: Wingspan Press, 2010), 62.

19. Gilbert, *The Most Secret War*, 36.

20. "US Army Special Electronic Mission Aircraft Units," INSCOM History Files, 3-5; Gilbert, *The Most Secret War*, 114.

21. "US Army Special Electronic Mission Aircraft Units," 3-5; Gilbert, *The Most Secret War*, 95.

22. United States Department of the Army Lineage and Honors, 224th Military Intelligence Battalion, INSCOM Historical Files, 3; "US Army Special Electronic Mission Aircraft Units," 3-5; Buley Papers, "ASA Organizations in Vietnam," 6; Interview, 2d Lieutenant Richard K. Willard, Assistant USARPAC Historian, with Lieutenant Colonel Robert L. Swanson, 3 June 1971, subject: Historical Interview of Lieutenant Colonel Swanson, INSCOM Historical Files (hereafter cited as Swanson Interview), 1; Gilbert, *The Most Secret War*, 95.

23. Swanson Interview, 1.

24. Gilbert, *The Most Secret War*, 59-60.

25. Buley Papers, "US Army Vietnam ARDF Units," 1-4; "Milestones in Development of US Army Tactical EW Support," INSCOM Historical Files, 6; "CRAZY CAT/CEFLIEN LION," INSCOM Historical Files, 1; "Airborne Collection Information Paper," INSCOM Historical Files, 1; "US Army Special Electronic Mission Aircraft Units," 4-5; The 1st RR Company sent one of its remaining RP-2E Neptune aircraft to Fort Rucker, Alabama, for permanent display at the Army Aviation Museum.

26. Gilbert, *The Most Secret War*, 114.

27. Buley Papers, "US Army Vietnam ARDF Units," 14.

28. Gilbert, *The Most Secret War*, 114.

29. Buley Papers, "US Army Vietnam ARDF Units," 16-18; "US Army Special Electronic Mission Aircraft Units," 6.

30. E. R. Johnson and Lloyd S. Jones, *American Military Transport Aircraft since 1925*, 401.

31. "Airborne Collection Information Paper"; "3d Military Intelligence Battalion," INSCOM Historical Files.

32. E. R. Johnson and Lloyd S. Jones, *American Military Transport Aircraft since 1925*, 435-436.

33. E-mail, John B. Hyde to Thomas Hauser, 2 September 2010. As a pilot in the 146th Aviation Company, Warrant Officer John B. Hyde was tasked to assess the South Vietnamese Air Force (VNAF) pilots who would fly RU-6A aircraft on ARDF missions in support of the South Vietnamese forces. His findings determined that "VNAF pilots were highly competent in the aircraft and the mission, limited only by equipment/political problems." Email, John B. Hyde to Thomas Hauser, 14 April 2010.

34. Gilbert, *The Most Secret War*, 96, 114.

35. Gilbert, *The Most Secret War*, 114.

36. Ibid.

37. Gilbert, *The Most Secret War*, 6; 144th Aviation Company Campaign Participation Credit, INSCOM Historical Files; Buley Papers, "US Army Vietnam ARDF Units," 9-11.

38. Memorialization of SEMA Personnel, INSCOM Historical Files.

39. Ibid.

40. E-mail, Clark L. Sullins to Thomas Hauser, 10 February 2016.

41. "US Army Special Electronic Mission Aircraft Units," 5-6; Interview, author with Lieutenant Colonel (Ret.) William C. Hauser, 25 March 2013, subject: MI Aviation Retrospective, INSCOM Historical Files (hereafter cited as Hauser Interview), 5.

42. Gilbert, *The Most Secret War*, 114.

43. Hauser Interview, 4; Gilbert, *The Most Secret War*, 96, 114.

44. "LEFT JAB," INSCOM Historical Files; Hauser Interview, 3-4.

45. "LEFT JAB," INSCOM Historical Files.

46. "LEFT JAB," INSCOM Historical Files; Hauser Interview, 3-5.

47. "LEFT JAB," INSCOM Historical Files.

48. "LEFT JAB," INSCOM Historical Files; "138th Military Intelligence Company (AE) History," INSCOM Historical Files.

49. "US Army Special Electronic Mission Aircraft Units," INSCOM Historical Files, 4.

50. "LEFT BANK (UH-1D/H)," INSCOM Historical Files, 1-3.

51. "LEFT BANK (UH-1D/H)," INSCOM Historical Files, 4-5; "LEFT BANK Incident Summary," INSCOM Historical Files.

52. Interview, author with Colonel (Retired) Carlos M. Collat, 3 June 2013, subject: MI Aviation Retrospective, INSCOM Historical Files (hereafter cited as Collat Interview), 1-2.

53. Collat Interview, 1-2; "LEFT BANK Information Paper," INSCOM Historical Files; "LEFT BANK (UH-1 D/H)," 7.

54. "LEFT BANK (UH-1 D/H)," 7.

55. Gilbert, *The Most Secret War*, 82.

56. "LEFT BANK (UH-1 D/H)," 9.

57. Collat Interview, 2; "Origins of the Army Security Agency and INSCOM," 8.

58. Al Adcock, *O-1 Bird Dog in Action* (Carrolton, TX: Squadron/Signal Publications, 1988), 32, 23.

59. Collat, "The History, the Legacy, and the Message of Army SEMA," 3-4.

60. Ibid.

61. Sergeant David Melancon, "Mohawks: pilots love to fly them, mechanics hate to fix them," *INSCOM Journal*, 13, no. 7 (September 1990) : 15.

62. Ibid.

63. Bill Gunston, *Aircraft of the Vietnam War* (Wellingborough, Northamptonshire: Patrick Stephens, 1987), 62; Collat Interview 3; Danny Johnson, "Grumman OV-1 Mohawk," 13; Chief Warrant Officer 3 Edward Jones, "Special Electronic Mission Aircraft: Intelligence from Above," 4.

64. Sergeant Michael Westerfield, "Mohawk Retires; one of the best passes the torch," Camp Humphreys News Release (23 September 1996), 3; Melancon, "Mohawks: pilots love to fly them, mechanics hate to fix them," 14-15.

65. Colonel William G. Benedict, et.al., "A Critical Analysis of US Army Intelligence Organizations and Concepts in Vietnam, 1965-1969," (Carlisle Barracks, PA: US Army War College, 8 March 1971) [Via Vietnam.ttu.edu], 137.

66. Buley Papers, "The Grumman OV-1 Mohawk," 1.

67. Buley Papers, The Grumman OV-1 Mohawk, INSCOM Historical Files, 2.

68. Collat, "The History, the Legacy and the Message of Army SEMA," 3; Reed, "Retiring the Mohawk – The End?" : 3.

69. Benedict, "A Critical Analysis of US Army Intelligence Organizations and Concepts in Vietnam, 1965-1969," 133.

70. Ibid.

71. Johnson, "Grumman OV-1 Mohawk," : 15; Gunston, *Aircraft of the Vietnam War*, 63; Erik Hildebrand, "Grumman OV-1 Mohawks at American Wings Air Museum," *Warbirds* 18, no. 3 (April 1995) : 16; Chief Warrant Officer 3 Edward Jones, "Special Electronic Mission Aircraft: Intelligence from Above," 3; Carlos M. Collat, "History of SEMA Briefing," 30 November 2004, slides 7 and 14.

72. Benedict, "A Critical Analysis of US Army Intelligence Organizations and Concepts in Vietnam, 1965-1969," 134.

73. Ibid.

74. Ibid., 142.

75. Buley Papers, "The Grumman OV-1 Mohawk," 2.

76. Gunston, *Aircraft of the Vietnam War*, 63; Collat, "The History, the Legacy and the Message of Army SEMA," 4; Reed, "Retiring the Mohawk – The End?" : 3.

77. Thomas Hauser, "INSCOM Flying High," *INSCOM Journal* 26, no. 1 (Fall 2003) : 22.

78. Ibid.

79. *The Mohawker: Newsletter of the OV-1 Mohawk Association*, Reunion Issue No. 3 (Summer 1991) : 3; Reed, "Retiring the Mohawk – The End?" : 3.

80. Left JAB Information Paper, INSCOM Historical Files, 2.

Chapter Three

1. Collat, "The History, the Legacy and the Message of Army SEMA," 12-13; LEFT JAB, 2.

2. The History of the 507th USASA Group, INSCOM Historical Files, 7; US Army Special Electronic Mission Aircraft Units, 7; Johnson, "Grumman OV-1 Mohawk," : 16; Alfred Price, *The History of US Electronic Warfare*, Volume II (Pikesville, MD: Port City Press, 1989), 312.

3. Norman J. Campbell, "GUARDRAIL: A Joint Tactical Sigint Support System," INSCOM Historical Files, 15.

4. Ibid.; Collat, GUARDRAIL Presentation, 16.

5. "The Guardrail Story: 20 Years and Seven Generations," INSCOM Historical Files, 1; Collat, GUARDRAIL Presentation, 18, 2; J. Daniel Sherman, "Lessons Learned from the Early Stages of Development of the Guardrail Common Sensor for the Radical Reduction of Cycle Time," *Acquisition Review Quarterly* (Summer 2003), 1.

6. Collat Interview, 3-5.

7. "The Guardrail Story," 2; Collat, GUARDRAIL Presentation, 18-19.

8. ASA Historical Summary, fiscal year 1973; Buley Papers, "The Beginning, Part II," 11.

9. Hauser Interview, 6.

10. Collat, "The History, the Legacy and the Message of Army SEMA," 18; Hauser Interview, 6; Interview, author with Colonel (Ret.) Robert Pitman, 9 July 2012, subject: 3d MI Battalion and SEMA History, INSCOM Historical Files (hereafter cited as Pitman Interview), 2.

11. Pitman Interview, 2-3.

12. Hauser Interview, 6-7; Collat Interview, 4.

13. Campbell, "GUARDRAIL: A Joint Tactical Sigint Support System," 16; Critical Communications Information Paper, INSCOM Historical Files, 52-53.

14. Buley Papers, "US Army Special Electronic Mission Aircraft Units," 8; History of the 330th ASA Company (untitled), INSCOM Historical Files, 3; GUARDRAIL IIA Information Paper, INSCOM Historical Files, 2; GO 276, Headquarters, United States Army Security Agency, 8 November 1973, effective 5 November; GUARDRAIL IIA Information Paper, INSCOM Historical Files, 2; Collat Interview, 4.

15. Campbell, "GUARDRAIL: A Joint Tactical Sigint Support System,"15; ASA Historical Summary, fiscal year 1973, 139; GUARDRAIL IV, INSCOM Historical Files, 1; Buley Papers, Post-Vietnam Era Systems, INSCOM Historical Files, 2.

16. GUARDRAIL IV, 1-2.

17. Finnegan and Danysh, *Military Intelligence*, 174.

18. 138th Military Intelligence Company (AE) History, INSCOM Historical Files, 1.

Chapter Four

1. Interview, author with Lieutenant Colonel (Ret.) Douglas Roberts, 13 June 2013, subject: MI Aviation Retrospective, INSCOM Historical Files (hereafter cited as Roberts Interview), 10.

2. Donald Oberdorfer, *The Two Koreas: A Contemporary History* (New York: Basic Books, 2001), 10.

3. Oberdorfer, *The Two Koreas: A Contemporary History*, 47-48, 75. DPRK had actually attempted several assassination plots against Park Chung Hee in the 1960s and 1970s.

4. Interview, author with Colonel (Ret.) Darell G. Lance, 27 October 2011, subject: Aviation Career Retrospective, Part II, INSCOM Historical Files (hereafter cited as Lance Interview II), 3; Interview, author with Colonel (Ret.) Darell G. Lance, 27 October 2011, subject: Aviation Career Retrospective, Part I, INSCOM Historical Files (hereafter cited as Lance Interview I), 3.

5. Interview, author with Chief Warrant Officer 4 (Ret.) Michael Bunty, 30 March 2012, subject: GUARDRAIL Retrospective, Part II, INSCOM Historical Files (hereafter cited as Bunty Interview II), 6, 2.

6. INSCOM Annual Historical Review, fiscal year 1977, INSCOM Historical Files, 100; Lance Interview I, 3-4.

7. Lance Interview I, 3-4, 9; 146th Army Security Agency Company (Aviation) Historical Report, fiscal year 1978, INSCOM Historical Files, 10.

8. 146th Army Security Agency Company (Aviation) GUARDRAIL IV Historical Report, fiscal year 1977, INSCOM Historical Files,15; Interview, author with Chief Warrant Officer 4 (Ret.) Michael Bunty, 23 March 2012, subject: GUARDRAIL Retrospective, Part I, INSCOM Historical Files (hereafter cited as Bunty Interview I), 10.

9.   Interview, Dr. Douglas V. Johnson II with Lieutenant General (Ret.) Donald L. Kerrick, no date, subject: Oral History, INSCOM Historical Files (hereafter cited as Kerrick Interview), 56; Bunty Interview I, 4.

10. Lance Interview I, 2-3.

11. Ibid., 9.

12. 146th Army Security Agency Company (Aviation) GUARDRAIL IV Historical Report, fiscal year 1977, INSCOM Historical Files, 16; Interview, author with Chief Warrant Officer 4 (Ret.) Michael Bunty, 26 April 2012, subject: GUARDRAIL Retrospective, Part III, INSCOM Historical Files (hereafter cited as Bunty Interview III), 5, 15.

13. Bunty Interview II, 5.

14. Ibid., 16.

15. Bunty Interview I, 10; Pitman Interview, 1.

16. Bunty Interview III, 13; Thomas Hauser, "INSCOM Flying High," 22.

17. Pitman Interview, 2-3.

18. Bunty Interview I, 3.

19. Ibid., 3-4.

20. Lance Interview I, 8.

21. Ibid., 8.

22. Lance Interview I, 2; Bunty Interview II, 2.

23. INSCOM Annual Historical Review, fiscal year 1977, INSCOM Historical Files, 134.

24. INSCOM Annual Historical Review, fiscal year 1977, INSCOM Historical Files, 17; Bunty Interview I, 6.

25. Bunty Interview III, 1.

26. Ibid.

27. 146th Army Security Agency Company (Aviation) GUARDRAIL IV Historical Report, fiscal year 1977, INSCOM Historical Files, 8.

Chapter Five

1. Captain Fred Hoffman, "The Role of Intelligence in President Jimmy Carter's Troop Withdrawal Decisions," in *Military Intelligence* 28, no. 1 (January-March 2002) : 29.

2. Office of the Deputy Chief of Staff for Intelligence and Threat Analysis Historical Report, fiscal year 1978, INSCOM Historical Files, 1. ITAC was established on 1 October 1977 as an interim organization and was not established permanently until 1 January 1978; Karen Kovach, "Imagery Intelligence and the Army," 21 January 2000, INSCOM Historical Files, 2-3.

3. Office of the Deputy Chief of Staff for Intelligence and Threat Analysis Historical Report, fiscal year 1978, INSCOM Historical Files, 8; North Korea Special Studies Team, The Combat Elements of the North Korea Army, Volume I, Order of Battle, Part 1, issued July 1979, I-3; North Korea Special Studies Team, The Combat Elements of the North Korean Army, Volume I, Order of Battle, Part 1, issued July 1979, presented the findings in official form, front matter.

4. "INSCOM and Its Heritage: An Organizational History of the Command and Its Units," 1985, INSCOM Historical Files, 69; 704th MIDAS Historical Report, fiscal year 1978, INSCOM Historical Files, 2.

5. 704th MIDAS Historical Report, fiscal year 1977, INSCOM Historical Files, 3; "INSCOM and Its Heritage," 69.

6. Ibid.

7. Frank J. Delear, *Helicopters and Airplanes of the U.S. Army* (New York: Dodd, Mead, and Co. 1977), 61; 704th MIDAS Historical Report, fiscal year 1978, INSCOM Historical Files, 9; Staff Sergeant Michael Westerfield, "Last of the Mohawks: After 36 years, Army's OV-1 Retires," *KORUS Monthly* 25, no.11 (November 1996) : 13.

8. *OV-1 Mohawk Survivability: How to Conduct Aerial Surveillance and Survive*, TC 30-79: 15 January 1976, 12; Captain William C. Weaver, "Mohawks in Hostile Airspace," *Military Intelligence* 7. No. 4 (October-December) 1981 : 52.

9. Chief Warrant Officer 3 Edward Jones, "Special Electronic Mission Aircraft: Intelligence from Above," 4; 704th MIDAS Historical Report, fiscal year 1978, INSCOM Historical Files, 3; 501st MI Group Briefing, INSCOM History Files, 6; Lieutenant Colonel Ballard M. Barker and Chief Warrant Officer 2 Rex A. Williams, "Side-Looking Airborne Radar: The Evolution of a System," *Military Intelligence* 7, no. 2 (April –June 1981) : 18-20.

10. Barker and Williams, "Side-Looking Airborne Radar: The Evolution of a System, 17"; Lance Interview I, 4; Captain Ted D. Whitley, "SLAR's I&W Peacekeeping Role in Korea," *Military Intelligence* 5, no. 2 (April-June 1979) : 54-55.

11. 501st MI Group Annual Historical Report, fiscal year 1978, vol. 2, INSCOM Historical Files, 23; 704th MIDAS Historical Report, fiscal year 1978, INSCOM Historical Files, 9, 2.

12. 1979 Director's Trophy Nominee: 146th ASA AVN Co (Fwd), 20-22, A-1, A-7.

13. North Korea Special Studies Team, The Combat Elements of the North Korean Army, Volume I Order of Battle, Part 1, issued July 1979, I-3; Oberdorfer, *The Two Koreas: A Contemporary History*, 102.

14. Oberdorfer, *The Two Koreas: A Contemporary History* 103; North Korea Special Studies Team, The Combat Elements of the North Korean Army, Volume I Order of Battle, Part 1, issued July 1979, II-1.

15. Office of the Deputy Chief of Staff for Intelligence and Threat Analysis Historical Report, fiscal year 1978, INSCOM Historical Files, 8.

16. 1979 Director's Trophy Nominee: 146th ASA AVN Co (Fwd), 9.

Works Cited

Interviews by the Author

Bunty, Michael

Collat, Carlos M.

Hauser, William C.

Lance, Darell G.

Pitman, Robert

Roberts, Douglas

Thomas, John D.

Other Interviews

Swanson, Robert L., Interview by Richard K. Willard, 3 June 1971, INSCOM Historical Files.

Repositories of Unpublished Sources

United States Army Intelligence and Security Command Cryptologic Records Repository and Command History Office Files.

Texas Tech University, Sam Johnson Vietnam Archive, Digital Materials.

Bibliography of Secondary Sources

Adcock, Al. *O-1 Bird Dog in Action*. Carrolton, TX: Squadron/Signal Publications, 1988.

Ball, Desmond. *Signals Intelligence (SIGINT) in South Korea*. Canberra, Australia: Australian National University, 1995.

Bonnet, Douglas W. *The Sentinel and the Shooter*. Livermore, CA: Wingspan Press, 2010.

Butler, Howard K. *Army Air Corps Airplanes and Observation: 1935-1941*. Saint Louis, MO: Historical Office, United States Aviation Systems Command, 1990.

Donald, David. *Spyplane: The Secret World of Aerial Intelligence Gathering*. London, UK: Aerospace Publishing Ltd., 1987.

Delear, Frank J. *Helicopters and Airplanes of the U.S. Army.* New York: Dodd, Mead, and Co., 1977.

Finnegan, John Patrick and Romana Danysh. *Military Intelligence.* Washington, DC: U.S. Army Center of Military History, 1998.

Gunston, Bill. *Aircraft of the Vietnam War.* Wellingborough, Northamptonshire, UK: Patrick Stephens, 1987.

Hennessy, Juliette A. *The United States Army Air Arm, April 1861 to April 1917.* Washington, DC: Office of Air Force History, United States Air Force, 1958.

Infield, Glenn B. *Unarmed and Unafraid: The First Complete History of the Men, Missions, Training, and Techniques of Aerial Reconnaissance.* London, The MacMillan Company, 1970.

Johnson, E.R. and Lloyd S. Jones. *American Military Transport Aircraft since 1925.* Jefferson, NC: McFarland and Company, Inc., 2013.

Koch, Brigadier General Oscar W. with Robert Hays. *G2: Intelligence for Patton.* Atglen, PA: Schiffer Publishing Ltd., 1999.

Maurer, Maurer. *The US Air Service in World War I.* Washington, DC: Office of Air Force History, 1978.

Oberdorfer, Donald. *The Two Koreas: A Contemporary History.* New York: Basic Books, 2001.

Price, Alfred. *The History of US Electronic Warfare*, Volume II. Pikesville, MD: Port City Press, 1989.

Raines, Edgar F. *Eyes of Artillery: The Origins of Modern U.S. Army Aviation in World War II.* Washington, D.C.: U.S. Army Center of Military History, 2000.

Raines, Rebecca Robbins. *Getting the Message Through: A Branch History of the U.S. Army Signal Corps*, Washington, DC: U.S. Army Center of Military History, 1995.

Stacy, William E. *US Army Border Operations in Germany, 1945-1983.* Heidelberg, Germany: U.S. Army Europe, 1984.

Stanton, Shelby L. *U.S. Army and Allied Ground Forces in Vietnam Order of Battle.* Washington, DC: US News Books, 1981.

Works Cited

Published Articles

Barker, Ballard M. and Rex A. Williams. "Side-Looking Airborne Radar: The Evolution of a System." *Military Intelligence,* 7, no. 2 (April –June 1981) : 17-20.

Campbell, William H. "One of a Kind." *Soldiers*, 33, no. 6 (June 1978) : 25-26.

Choice, Dena. "14,135 Hours, 0 Accidents and Still Flying High." *INSCOM Journal,* 10, no. 1 (January-February 1987) : 28.

Fischer, Joan E. "Thanks for the Memories." *INSCOM Journal,* 19, no. 6 (November-December 1996) : 26-27.

Gordon, Donald. "CEWI Battalion: Intelligence and Electronic Warfare on the Battlefield." *Military Intelligence*, 5, no. 4 (October-December 1979) : 22-28.

Hauser, Thomas. "INSCOM Flying High." *INSCOM Journal,* 26, no. 1 (Fall 2003) : 22-23.

Hildebrand, Erik. "Grumman OV-1 Mohawks at American Wings Air Museum." *Warbirds,* 18, no. 3 (April 1995).

Hoffman, Frederick. "The Role of Intelligence in President Jimmy Carter's Troop Withdrawal Decisions." *Military Intelligence,* 28, no. 1 (January-March 2002) : 28-30.

Johnson, Daniel. "Grumman OV-1 Mohawk." *On Point: The Journal of Army History,* 11, no. 2 (Fall 2005) : 12.

Jones, Edward. "Special Electronic Mission Aircraft: Intelligence from Above." *United States Army Aviation Digest*, 27, no. 4 (April 1981) : 3-9.

McGarvey, Barbara. "Nothing is Impossible for the 'Eyes of USAREUR.'" *INSCOM Journal,* 4, no. 6 (July 1981) : 2-5.

Melancon, David. "Mohawks: pilots love to fly them, mechanics hate to fix them." *INSCOM Journal*, 13, no. 7 (September 1990) : 14-15.

Rankin, R. E. "Army Reservists Enjoy Two Worlds." *The Newspaper* (Orlando, Florida). 27 July 1977, 1a.

Reed, Paul. "Retiring the Mohawk – The End?" Mohawk Retirement Ceremony Speech. *Mohawker Newsletter,* no. 25 (no date) : 1-4.

Sotham, John. "The Last of the Mohawks: Grumman's Triple-tail, Bug-eyed, Heat-seeking Camera Platform." *Air and Space Magazine,* 11, no. 6 (March 1997) : 54.

Weaver, William. "Mohawks in Hostile Airspace." *Military Intelligence,* 7, no. 4 (October-December 1981) : 49-52.

Westerfield, Michael. "Last of the Mohawks: After 36 years, Army's OV-1 Retires." *KORUS Monthly,* 25, no.11 (November 1996) : 10-13.

Whitley, Theodore D. "SLAR's I&W Peacekeeping Role in Korea." *Military Intelligence,* 5, no. 2 (April-June 1979) : 54-55.

Index